POETIC ORIGINS
AND THE BALLAD

THE MACMILLAN COMPANY
NEW YORK · BOSTON · CHICAGO · DALLAS
ATLANTA · SAN FRANCISCO

MACMILLAN & CO., LIMITED
LONDON · BOMBAY · CALCUTTA
MELBOURNE

THE MACMILLAN CO. OF CANADA, LTD.
TORONTO

POETIC ORIGINS AND THE BALLAD

BY

LOUISE POUND, Ph.D.

Professor of English in the University of Nebraska

New York

THE MACMILLAN COMPANY

1921

TO

HARTLEY AND NELLIE ALEXANDER

PREFACE

The leading theses of the present volume are that the following assumptions which have long dominated our thought upon the subject of poetic origins and the ballads should be given up, or at least should be seriously qualified; namely, belief in the " communal " authorship and ownership of primitive poetry; disbelief in the primitive artist; reference to the ballad as the earliest and most universal poetic form; belief in the origin of narrative songs in the dance, especially definition of the English and Scottish traditional ballad type as of dance origin; belief in the emergence of traditional ballads from the illiterate, that is, belief in the communal creation rather than *re-creation* of ballads; belief in the special powers of folk-improvisation; and belief that the making of traditional ballads is a " closed account." The papers making it up are reprinted, with a few modifications and considerable additional material, from the *Publications of the Modern Language Association of America,* from *Modern Philology,* from *The Mid-West Quarterly,* and from *Modern Language Notes.* A few are printed for the first time, and the chapter on " Balladry in America " is indebted to a chapter on " Oral Literature in America " published in *The Cambridge History of American Literature.* Thanks are due to the publishers for permission to utilize passages from the latter. The polemical tone of the papers, which is so marked as to need explanation, is to be accounted for by the fact that each was written to urge a distinctive point of view or to oppose some accepted position, i. e., was a piece of special pleading. It was impossible to eliminate the argumentative note without re-writing the articles *in toto*.

Much attention is given in the course of the volume to the subject of folk-song in America.

The author wishes to express grateful acknowledgment to Professor H. M. Belden of the University of Missouri, who first encouraged her to interest herself in the study of folk-song, and to Professor H. B. Alexander of the University of Nebraska, to whom she owes her interest in poetic origins and in much more besides. Both have read the manuscript in parts and to both she is indebted for generous assistance. Adequate acknowledgment of their help cannot be dismissed with a phrase.

LOUISE POUND.

University of Nebraska.

CONTENTS

CONTENTS

POETIC ORIGINS AND THE BALLAD

CHAPTER I

THE BEGINNINGS OF POETRY

Certain [Indian] societies require that each member have a special song; this song is generally of the man's own composition, although sometimes these songs are inherited from a father or a near relative who when living had been a member of the society. These individual songs are distinct from songs used in the ceremonies and regarded as the property of the society, although the members are entitled to sing them on certain occasions. When this society holds its formal meetings a part of the closing exercises consists of the simultaneous singing by all the members present of their individual songs. The result is most distressing to a listener, but there are no listeners unless by chance an outsider is present, for each singer is absorbed in voicing his own special song which is strictly his own personal affair, so that he pays no attention to his neighbour, consequently the pandemonium to which he contributes does not exist for him.

The foregoing paragraph from Miss Alice C. Fletcher's account of Indian music [1] reads like a travesty of the accepted view of primitive song, its character and authorship. There is the familiar primitive "horde," engaged in festal singing, without onlookers. Yet instead of col-

[1] *The Study of Indian Music.* Reprinted from the *Proceedings of the National Academy of Sciences*, vol. I, p. 233. 1915. According to Miss Fletcher, the Indians are sitting as they sing.

Compare a custom among the Karok, an Indian tribe of California (Stephen Powers, *Contributions to North American Ethnology*, vol. III, p. 29, Washington, 1877).

laborative composition, improvisation, and communal ownership of the ensuing " ballad," we have individual authorship and ownership, and individual singing. This is the testimony of a specialist who has spent many years among the people of whom she writes, studying and recording their songs and their modes of composition. Easily recognizable is the homogeneous primitive group, singing in festal ceremony; but this group does not conduct itself in the way which literary historians have insisted that we should expect.

The songs of primitive peoples have received much attention in recent years, especially the songs of the American Indians. An immense amount of material has been collected and made available; and this has been done in a scientific way, with the help of countless phonographic and other records. Instead of having to rely on the stray testimonies of travellers, explorers, historians, and essayists, the student of primitive poetry has now at his disposal an amount of data unavailable to his predecessors. He need not linger among the fascinating mysteries of romantic hypotheses, but can supply himself with the carefully observed facts of scientific record.[2]

In this matter it cannot be valid to object that we should not look among North or South American Indians, or Eski-

[2] References of chief importance for the American Indians are Frederick R. Burton, *American Primitive Music*, with especial attention to the songs of the Ojibways, New York, 1909; Natalie Curtis, *The Indian's Book*, New York, 1900; and the following thorough studies: Frances Densmore, *Chippewa Music*, in Bulletins 45 (1910) and 53 (1913) of the *Bureau of American Ethnology*, and *Teton Sioux Music*, Washington (1918); Alice C. Fletcher, *A Study of Omaha Indian Music*, Papers of the Peabody Museum, vol. I, No. 5, 1893, *Indian Story and Song*, Boston, 1900, *The Hako: a Pawnee*

mos for " beginnings." It cannot reasonably be said that these trib?s?re too advanced, too highly civilized, to afford trustworthy evidence as to aboriginal modes. As a matter of fact, we can go little farther back, in the analysis of culture, than these people, if we are to stay by what can be demonstrated. When we have learned what we can learn from the primitive tribes on our own continent, in South America, Africa, Australia, Oceania, we know very nearly all that we can surely know. If we go to the prehistoric, we are conjecturing, and we ought to label our statements " conjecture." In general, gradations of " primitiveness " among savage peoples are difficult to make. A social group may show the simplest or least organized social structure, and yet be relatively advanced in musical and artistic talent. Another group may show advance in social organization, yet be backward in song and story. And certainly even the most advanced of the Indian communities (with the exception of civilized Mexico and Peru) are every whit as primitive as the mediæval peasant communes, from whose supposed ways we are constantly asked to learn as regards poetic beginnings.[3] If, as we

Ceremony, 22 Report (1904), *Bureau of American Ethnology*, and *The Study of Indian Music* quoted *supra;* James Mooney, *The Ghost-Dance Religion*, 14 Report, *Bureau of Ethnology*, Part II, 1896. Excellent pieces of work are " Hopi Songs " and " Zuñi Melodies," by B. I. Gilman, published respectively in the *Journal of American Ethnology and Archæology*, vol. I, 1891, and vol. v, 1908, but nothing is said in these regarding the composition or presentation of the songs recorded. Many references are cited later, especially books, studies, or special articles dealing with South American, African, and Australian tribes.

[3] See F. B. Gummere, *The Beginnings of Poetry*, 1901, and *The Popular Ballad*, 1907. See also *Primitive Poetry and the Ballad, Modern Philology*, I, 1904.

are told, prehistoric song-modes are reflected in the folk-dances and festal throngs of mediæval peasants and villagers, or in the singing of nineteenth-century Corsican field laborers, Styrian threshers, Gascon vintage choruses, Italian country-folk, Silesian peasants, Faroe Island fishermen, and harvest-field songs everywhere,[4] they ought to be reflected yet more in the song-modes of the American Indians.

I — " COMMUNAL " AUTHORSHIP AND OWNERSHIP

At the present time the accepted or orthodox view, *i. e.,* among literary critics, hardly among anthropologists, concerning the authorship of primitive song and the " beginnings of poetry " is reflected in such passages as the following, from a recent work by Professor Richard Green Moulton:[5]

The primary element of literary form is the ballad dance. This is the union of verse with musical accompaniment and dancing; the dancing being, not exactly what the words suggest to modern ears, but the imitative and suggestive action of which an orator's gestures are the nearest survival. Literature, where it first appears spontaneously, takes this form: a theme or story is at once versified, accompanied with music, and suggested in action. When the Israelites triumphed at the Red Sea, Miriam "took a timbrel in her hands; and all the women went out after her with timbrels and dances." This was a ballad dance; it was a more elaborate example of the same when David, at the inauguration of Jerusalem, " danced before the Lord with all his might." And writers who deal with literary origins offer abundant illus-

[4] *Ibid.*
[5] *The Modern Study of Literature*, Chicago, 1915.   From Chapter I, " The Elements of Literary Form."

trations of folk-dances among the most diverse peoples in an early stage of civilization.

In this passage and in his diagrams showing literary evolution [6] Professor Moulton gives the "ballad dance" the initial position in the chronology of musical and literary history, characterizing it as the "primitive literary form"— the ballad dance, moreover, according to the usual view, of the *throng*. Individual composition of and proprietorship in song is of secondary development; and when this stage has been reached, "folk-song" has passed into "artistry."

The following passages make clear the position of Professor A. S. Mackenzie [7]: "Inasmuch as dancing is the most spontaneous of all the arts, it may be regarded as the earliest. Linked with inarticulate vocal cries it fell under the spell of measure or order, and slowly grew more rational" . . . "impulsive motions and sounds prepare the way for voluntary movements of the body and

[6] *Ibid.*, pp. 18, 26.

[7] *The Evolution of Literature*, 1911. For the quotations cited, see pp. 131, 147, 261, 263.

This view of the priority of the dance and of the dance song is found in Franz Böhme's *Geschichte des Tanzes im Deutschland* (1888): "Tanzlieder waren die ersten Lieder," "Beim Tänze wurden die ältesten epischen Dichtungen (erzählende Volkslieder) gesungen," "Die älteste Poesie eines jeden Volkes ist eine Verbindung von Tanz, Spiel und Gesang."

Karl Bücher, *Arbeit und Rhythmus* (2nd ed. 1899), finds the origin of poetry in labor songs, and assigns to primitive labor the rôle so often assigned to the primitive dance: ". . . es ist die energische, rhythmische Körperbewegung, die zur Entstehung der Poesie geführt hat, insbesondere diejenige Bewegung, welche wir Arbeit nennen. Es gilt dies aber ebensowohl von der formellen als der materiellen Seite der Poesie," p. 306.

the voice. When these are controlled by rhythm, the rudiments of dancing and music have emerged, though they remain inseparable for many a year " . . . " It was such extemporaneous efforts [tribal improvisation] that gave rise to the first verses which bear any resemblance to what we are accustomed to call poetry. The first artist served his apprenticeship as an improviser under festal stimulus, before he learned to compose more worthy verse in retirement. Not only among the higher tribes but even in Europe the primitive custom of extemporizing coexists alongside the more advanced custom of composing with deliberation apart from the throng " . . . " His [primitive man's] humble verse is in constant dependence upon the collective emotion produced by the choric dance " . . . " Apart from the festal dance it is difficult to find any definite traces either of poetic sources or of poetic forms, and we are driven to the conclusion that the earliest art impulse is essentially collective rather than individual, objective rather than subjective. No doubt primitive improvisation is the halting keynote of individuality, but it is speedily lost in the ethnic chorus. In vain do we look here for that poetry which is born of meditation in solitude and deliberately framed into metrical perfection."

Last, let some passages from Professor Gummere's *The Beginnings of Poetry* be cited. Professor Gummere was recognized as a leading scholar of the subject, and in view of his learning, ability, and his years of attention to the matter, his words may well have especial weight. Here are some characteristic sentences [8]: " Poetry begins

8 *The Beginnings of Poetry* (1901), pp. 139, 321, 106, 212, 13, 93, etc. Later, by Professor Gummere, are *The Popular Ballad* (1907), and the chapter on Ballads in the *Cambridge History of English.*

with the impersonal, with communal emotion." " The ballad is a song made in the dance, and so by the dance. . . . The communal dance is the real source of the song." " The earliest 'muse' was the rhythm of the throng." " Festal throngs, not a poet's solitude, are the birthplace of poetry." " Overwhelming evidence shows all primitive poetical expression of emotion to have been collective." Let two quotations of greater length be given:

As the savage laureate slips from the singing, dancing crowd, which turns audience for the nonce, and gives his short improvisation, only to yield to the refrain of the chorus, so the actual habit of individual composition and performance has sprung from the choral composition and performance. The improvisations and the recitative are short deviations from the main road, beginnings of artistry, which will one day become journeys of the solitary singer over pathless hills of song, those " wanderings of thought" which Sophocles has noted; and the curve of evolution in the artist's course can show how rapidly and how far this progress has been made. But the relation must not be reversed; and if any fact seems established for primitive life, it is the precedence of choral song and dance. . . .

Here it is enough to show that rhythmical verse came directly from choral song, and that neither the choral song, nor any regular song, could have come from the recitative.

It is natural for one person to speak, or even to sing, and for ninety-nine persons to listen. It is also natural for a hundred persons, under strong emotion, to shout, sing, dance, in concert and as a throng, not as a matter of active and passive, of give and take, but in common consent of expression. The second situation . . . must have preceded.[9]

Literature (1908); but these deal primarily with the English and Scottish ballads, not with the origins of poetry.

[9] Pp. 80, 81. In Professor Gummere's article on " The Ballad and Communal Poetry," Child Memorial volume (Harvard Studies and Notes, etc., 1896), he said: " Spontaneous composition in a danc-

He reminds us again in an article on Folk-Song [10] that
" It is very important to remember that primitive man
regarded song as a momentary and spontaneous thing."

To come farther down in the history of song, a favorite
picture with Professor Gummere is of European peasant
folk in the Middle Ages, improvising " ballads " in song
and dance, and thus — by virtue of the simple homogene-
ous character of their life — establishing a type of balladry
superior to, and having more vitality than, anything of

ing multitude — all singing, all dancing, and all able on occasion
to improvise — is a fact of primitive poetry about which we may
be as çertain as such questions allow us to be certain. Behind
individuals stands the human horde. . . . An insistent echo of this
throng . . . greets us from the ballads." He added communal
poetry to Wundt's (*Ueber Ziele und Wege der Völkerpsychologie*)
three products of the communal mind,— speech, myth, and custom.
" Universality of the poetic gift among inferior races, spontaneity
or improvisation under communal conditions, the history of refrain
and chorus, the *early relation of narrative songs to the dance* " [the
italics are added] are facts so well established that " it is no absur-
dity to insist on the origin of poetry under communal and not
under artistic conditions." More difficulty lies in " the assertion
of *simultaneous composition.* Yet this difficulty is more apparent
than real."

Grosse, *Anfänge der Kunst* (1894), ch. ix, finds the poetry of
primitive peoples to be egoistic in inspiration, and gives examples
of lyrics of various types which point to this. " Im Allgemeinen
trägt die Lyrik der Jägervölker einen durchaus egoistischen Cha-
rakter. Der Dichter besingt seine persönlichen Leiden und Freu-
den; das Schicksal seiner Mitmenschen entlockt ihm nur selten
einen Ton." For Professor Gummere's discussion and rejection of
Grosse's view, see *The Beginnings of Poetry*, pp. 381 ff.

For a present-day German view of primitive poetry, see Erich
Schmidt, " Die Anfänge der Literatur," *Die Kultur der Gegenwart*,
Leipzig (1906), 1, pp. 1–27. For a French view, see A. van Gennep,
La Formation des Légendes, Paris (1910), pp. 210–211.

[10] In Warner's *Library of the World's Best Literature.*

the kind having its origin in individual authorship. It is a long gap, that between aboriginal song and dance and the English and Scottish ballads of the fifteenth and sixteenth centuries; yet it is a gap we are asked to bridge. Undoubtedly, if that "most ancient of creative processes," the communal throng chorally creating its song from the festal dance, existed among the mediæval peasants and produced work of the high value of the English and Scottish ballads, the same "ancient method" should prevail among that yet more primitive people, the American Indians.

That it is an absurd chronology which assumes that individuals have choral utterance before they are lyrically articulate   as   individuals,   seems — extraordinarily enough — to have little weight with theorists of this school. Did primitive man sing, dance, and compose in a throng, while he was yet unable to do so as an individual? We are asked to believe this. Are we to assume that he was inarticulate and without creative gift till suddenly he participated in some festal celebration and these gifts became his? Professor Gummere cites as evidence, so important as to deserve italics, Dr. Paul Ehrenreich's statement concerning the Botocudos of South America, "*They never sing without dancing, never dance without singing, and have but one word to express both song and dance.*" [11] Much the same thing, save as regards limitations of vocabulary, might have been said by a traveller among the ancient Greeks, with whom dance was generally inseparable from music and verse. Nothing is proved by this

[11] *Ueber die Botocuden, Zeitschrift für Ethnologie*, xix, pp. 30 ff. Quoted in *The Beginnings of Poetry*, p. 95; also *Democracy and Poetry* (1911), pp. 231 ff. See note 45, *infra*, p. 26.

characteristic of the Botocudos, if it is a characteristic; any more than anything is proved by the fact that the far more aboriginal Akkas of South Africa [12] have songless dances, or by the fact that danceless songs — a circumstance hard to fit into the accepted view of primitive poetry — have been reported among the Andamanese, the Australians, the Maori of New Zealand, Semang of Malaysia, Seri of Mexico, and Eskimo of the Arctic, as well as among practically all North American tribes that have been studied in detail. According to the testimony of Miss Fletcher, there are many songs sung by Indian societies in which there is no dancing.[13] Such songs are spoken of as "Rest Songs." In the account quoted at the opening of this volume, of the simultaneous singing of individual songs by the members of a certain society as the closing act of a meeting, the members are sitting as they sing. Their individual songs are, in a sense, credentials of membership. Each song is strictly individual, and refers to a personal experience. "In most societies," says Miss Fletcher, "as well as in the ceremonies of the tribe, the songs are led by a choir, or by persons officially ap-

[12] Some references for the Akkas are G. Burrows, *On the Natives of the Upper Welle District of the Belgian Congo*, *Journal of the Anthropological Institute* (1889), xxviii; Sir H. James, *Geographical Journal*, xvii, p. 40, 1906; G. A. Schweinfurth, *Heart of Africa*, N. Y., 1874, vol. ii; H. von Wissmann, *Meine Zweite Durchquerung Aequatorial-Afrikas*, Frankfort, 1890; H. M. Stanley, *In Darkest Africa*, N. Y., 1891; H. Schlichter, *Pygmy Tribes of Africa*, *Scot. Geog. Mag.*, viii, etc.

[13] In a letter to the author.

Among the Brazilian cannibal tribe, the Boros, the tribesman with a grievance enters the principal dance, stalks to a position in sight of all, and chants his solo standing stock still, with upraised hand. T. Whiffen, *The North-West Amazons* (1915), p. 196.

pointed as leaders.   The members of the society frequently join in the song.   I do not recall anyone performing a dramatic dance and singing at the same time.   While all dances are accompanied by song, many songs are sung without dancing.   Some of the dancing is not violent in action, the movement is merely rhythm and swaying.   In such dances, the dancers sing as they move.   Occasionally, as I recall, the song for a dance which is dramatic and vigorous, bringing all the body into play, will be sung by the choir (men and women seated about the drum).   Some of the people sitting and watching the dance may clap their hands in rhythm with the drum.   This, however, is play-fulness by some privileged person and indicates enjoy-ment."

Surely the individual does everything he can do, or chooses to do, as an individual, before, or contemporary with, his ability to do the same as a member of a throng. The testimonies of travellers as to communal singing and dancing among savage or peasant communities prove noth-ing at all as to origins; certainly they do not prove that collective poetic feeling and authorship preceded individ-ual feeling and authorship.   Testimonies as to tribal song ought to outnumber testimonies as to individual song, since the spectator is chiefly interested in tribal ways. He would be struck by and record tribal ceremonies, rit-uals, and songs, where individual singing would escape attention or seem unimportant.   Besides, choruses would no doubt be more numerous than solos, and bound up with more important occasions; much as solo dances are infre-quent, among savage tribes, compared to mass dancing. To reiterate, however, testimony no matter how great its quantity, that savage peoples sing and dance in throngs, or improvise while doing so, proves nothing as to the priority of communal over individual feeling, authorship, and ownership.

The evidence concerning primitive song which should have greatest weight is not that of travellers and explorers, interested chiefly in other things than song, but that of special scholars, who have recorded and studied available material with a view to its nature, its composition, and its vitality. Among these there seems to be neither doubt nor divergence of opinion; and their testimony is at variance with the now established tradition of the literary historian. The general social inspiration of song is not to be denied. In a broad sense, all art is a social phenomenon — the romanticists to the contrary. Song is mainly a social thing at the present time, and it was yet more prevailingly social among our remote ancestors. Rather is it proposed to subject to examination the following specific hypotheses: the inseparableness of primitive dance, music, and song; the simultaneous mass-composition of primitive song; mass-ownership of primitive song; the narrative character of primitive song; the non-existence of the primitive artist. Far from certain, also, is the hypothesis of the birth of rhythmic or musical utterance from rhythmic action, if this be conceived as a form of limb or bodily motion.

In citations of illustrative material, primary use is made of American Indian material. It is this material, on the whole, which has been collected and studied most carefully. Coming as it does from homogenous primitive peoples, in the tribal state, having one standard of life, and as yet unaffected by the poetic modes of civilization, it should have importance for the questions under discussion.   Parallel material — of which liberal use is made — available from South America, Africa, Australia, and Oceania, yields, however, the same evidence.

II — INDIVIDUAL AUTHORSHIP AND OWNERSHIP

That American Indian song is of individual composition, not the product of group improvisation, much evidence may be brought to support.   It will be seen also, from the illustrative material cited, that the Indian has a feeling of private ownership in his song.   It would be reasonable, therefore, to assume that, as far back as we can go in primitive society, there should be a sense of individual skill in song-making, as of individual skill in running, hurling a dart, leaping, or any other human activities. There is something absurd in singling out musical utterance as the one form of expression having only social origin or social existence.

A large number of Indian songs are said to have come into the mind of the Indian when he was in a dream or a trance (surely not a " communal " form of experience!).

Many of the Chippewa songs, for example, are classified as " dream songs."   Says Miss Densmore: [14]

Many Indian songs are intended to exert a strong mental influence, and dream songs are supposed to have this power in greater degree than any others.   The supernatural is very real to the Indian.   He puts himself in communication with it by fasting or by physical suffering.   While his body is thus subordinated to his mind a song occurs to him.   In after years he believes that

[14] Frances Densmore, *Chippewa Music*, I, II.   Bulletin 45 (1910) and 53 (1913), *Bureau of American Ethnology*.   For examples see I, pp. 118 ff., II, pp. 37 ff.   Also *Teton Sioux Music*, Bulletin 61 (1918), p. 60.

by singing this song he can recall the condition under which it
came to him — a condition of direct communication with the
supernatural.[15]

It is said that in the old days all the important songs were
"composed in dreams," and it is readily understood that the man
who sought a dream desired power superior to that he possessed.
A song usually came to a man in his "dream"; he sang this song
in the time of danger or necessity in the belief that by so doing he
made more potent the supernatural aid vouchsafed to him in the
dream. Songs composed, or received, in this manner were used
on the warpath, in the practice of medicine, and in any serious
undertaking of life.[16]

Compare also: "There is no limit to the number of
these [ghost-dance songs] as every trance at every dance
produces a new one, the trance subject after regaining
consciousness embodying his experience in the spirit
world in the form of a song, which is sung at the next
dance and succeeding performance until superseded by
other songs originating in the same way. Thus a single
dance may easily result in twenty or thirty new songs." [17]
Testimony from Australia is contributed by A. W. How-
itt: "In the tribes with which I have acquaintance, I
find it to be a common belief that the songs, using that
word in its widest meaning, as including all kinds of
aboriginal poetry, are obtained by the bards from the
spirits of the deceased, usually of their kindred, during
sleep, in dreams. . . . The Birraark professed to receive
his poetic inspiration from the Mrarts, as well as the ac-
companying dances, which he was supposed to have seen

[15] *Ibid.*, I, p. 118.

[16] *Ibid.*, II, p. 16.

[17] James Mooney, *The Ghost Dance Religion*, 14 report Bureau
of Ethnology, Part II (1896), p. 952. Many trance songs from
many tribes are given, pp. 953–1101.

first in ghost land. . . . In the Narrang-ga tribe there are
old men who profess to learn songs and dances from de-
parted spirits. These men are called Gurildras. . . . In
the Yuin tribe some men received their songs in dreams,
others when waking." Specimen songs are cited.[18]

There is also abundant testimony as to private owner-
ship. The following is from Le Jeune's *Relation* (1636):
"Let us begin with the feasts of the Savages. They have
one for war. At this they sing and dance in turn, accord-
ing to age; if the younger ones begin, the old men pity
them for exposing themselves to the ridicule of others.
Each has his own song, that another dare not sing lest he
give offense. For this very reason they sometimes strike
up a tune that belongs to their enemies to aggravate
them." [19] Of the Melanesians of British New Guinea we
are told that their songs and dances are " strictly copy-
right." " The only legitimate manner for people to ob-
tain the right to a dance or song not their own was to buy
it." [20] Private ownership of songs prevails also among
the American Indians.

[18] *The Native Tribes of South-East Australia,* London (1904), p.
416.

[19] *Jesuit Relations,* Thwaites ed. Vol. IX, p. 111.

[20] C. G. Seligman, *The Melanesians of British New Guinea* (1910),
p. 151. George Browne, *Melanesians and Polynesians* (1910) p.
451.

There are many testimonies to the existence of other primitive
artists beside the poet. Among the primitive Kwai or Bushmen, a
strong sense of individual talent in artistry is said to exist. " The
old Bushmen assert that the productions of an artist were always
respected as long as any recollection of him was preserved in his
tribe: during this period no one, however daring, would attempt to
deface his paintings by placing others over them. But when his
memory was forgotten, some aspirant after artistic fame appro-
priated the limited rock surface of the shelter, adapted for such a

The Chippewa have no songs which are the exclusive property of families or clans. Any young man may learn his father's songs, for example, by giving him the customary gift of tobacco, but he does not inherit the right to sing such songs, nor does his father force him to learn them.[21]

We learn further that the healer combines music and medicine. " If a cure of the sick is desired, he frequently mixes and rolls a medicine after singing the song which will make it effective." [22]   And that " The songs of a Chippewa doctor cannot be bought or sold." [23]

So far as the two men who heard me were concerned, the argument was convincing, but there lingered even with them a reluctance to help me with certain songs because they belonged to other persons. Nearly all the Indians of my acquaintance recognize this proprietary interest in songs. A has no right to sing B's songs; B did not compose them, but they came down to him through his family, or from some chief who fought him, and B alone should say whether they might be given another.[24]

Miss Fletcher writes of the Omaha:

It would be a mistake to fancy that songs floated indiscriminately about among the Indians, and could be picked up here and there by any chance observer. Every song had originally

display of talent, for his own performances, and unceremoniously painted over the efforts of those who preceded him. If we calculate that the memory of any artist would be preserved among his people for at least three generations, as every Bushman tribe prided itself on and boasted of the wall decorations of its chief cave, it would give a probable antiquity of about five hundred years to the oldest found in the Invani rock shelter." G. W. Stow, *The Native Races of South Africa* (1905), pp. 26, 27.

[21] *Chippewa Music*, I, p. 2.
[22] *Ibid.*, I, p. 20
[23] *Ibid.*, p. 119. See also *Teton Sioux Music*, p. 60.
[24] Burton, *American Primitive Music*, p. 118.

its owner. It belonged either to a society, secular or religious, to a certain clan or political organization, to a particular rite or ceremony, or to some individual. . . . The right to sing a song which belonged to an individual could be purchased, the person buying the song being taught it by the owner.

These beliefs and customs among the Indians have made it possible to preserve their songs without change from one generation to another. Many curious and interesting proofs of accuracy of transmittal have come to my knowledge during the past twenty years, while studying these primitive melodies. . . . Close and continued observation has revealed that the Indian, when he sings, is not concerned with the making of a musical presentation to his audience. He is simply pouring out his feelings, regardless of artistic effects. To him music is subjective: it is the vehicle of communication between him and the object of his desire.[25]

Now a few testimonies as to individual authorship. A first instance is from the songs of the Omaha. For the complete story of this song, the reader is referred to the account of Miss Fletcher:

At length the Leader stood up and said, " We have made peace, we have come in good faith, we will go forward, and Wa-kon'-da shall decide the issue." Then he struck up this song and led the way; and as the men and women followed, they caught the tune, and all sang it as they came near the Sioux village.[26]

[25] Alice C. Fletcher, *The Indian in Story and Song*, pp. 115–117.

[26] *Ibid.*, p. 22. The following passage from *A Study of Omaha Indian Music*, p. 25, by Alice C. Fletcher and Francis LaFlesche, also throws light on the composition of certain Indian songs:

Like the Poo-g'-thun, the Hae-thu-ska preserved the history of its members in its songs; when a brave deed was performed, the society decided whether it should be celebrated and without this dictate no man would dare permit a song to be composed in his honor. When a favorable decision was given, the task of composing the song devolved upon some man with musical talent. It has happened that the name of a man long dead has given place in a popular song to that of a modern warrior; this could only be done

Two instances from the Pawnee illustrate perfectly the poet musing in solitude on the meaning of nature,— like some Pawnee Wordsworth.

The " Song of the Bird's Nest " commemorates the story of a man who came upon a bird's nest in the grass:

He paused to look at the little nest tucked away so snug and warm, and noted that it held six eggs and that a peeping sound came from some of them. While he watched, one moved and soon a tiny bill pushed through the shell uttering a shrill cry. At once the parent birds answered and he looked up to see where they were. They were not far off; they were flying about in search of food, chirping the while to each other and now and then calling to the little ones in the nest. . . . After many days he desired to see the nest again. So he went to the place where he had found it and there it was as safe as when he had left it. But a change had taken place. It was now full to overflowing with little birds, who were stretching their wings, balancing on their little legs and making ready to fly, while the parents with encouraging calls were coaxing the fledglings to venture forth. " Ah! " said the man, " if my people would only learn of the birds, and like them, care for their young and provide for their future, homes would be full and happy, and our tribe strong and prosperous."

When this man became a priest, he told the story of the bird's nest and sang its song; and so it has come down to us as from the days of our fathers.[27]

The " Song of the Wren " was made by a priest who noted that the wren, the smallest and least powerful of the

by the consent of the society, which was seldom given, as the Omahas were averse to letting the memory of a brave man die. . . . the songs were transmitted from one generation to another with care, as was also the story of the deeds the songs commemorated.

[27] *The Hako, A Pawnee Ceremony*, in 22nd Report, *Bureau of American Ethnology*, Part II, p. 170. See also *The Indian in Story and Song*, p. 32, and Frances Densmore, *Teton Sioux Music*, p. 59.

birds, excelled them all in the fervor of its song. "Here," he thought, "is a teaching for my people. Everyone can be happy; even the most insignificant can have his song of thanks."

So he [the priest] made the story of the wren and sang it; and it has been handed down from that day,— a day so long ago no man can remember the time.[28]

Instances testifying to individual not communal composition of song among the Chippewa are no less easily cited.

The following explanation of a certain song was given by an Indian:

The song belonged to a certain man who sang it in the dances which were held before going to war. When this man was a boy he had a dream and in his dream he heard the trees singing as though they were alive: they sang that they were afraid of nothing except being blown down by the wind. When the boy awoke he made up this song, in which he repeats what he heard the trees say. The true meaning of the words is that there is no more chance of his being defeated on the warpath than there is that a tree will be blown down by the wind.[29]

The singer stated that he composed this song himself when he was a child. The circumstances were as follows: His mother had gone to a neighbor's, leaving him alone in the wigwam. He became very much afraid of the owl, which is the particular terror of all small Indians, and sang this song. It was just after sugar making and the wigwams were placed together beside the lake. The people in the other wigwams heard his little song. The melody was entirely new and it attracted them so that they learned it as he sang. The men took it up and used it in their moccasin games. For many years it was used in this way,

[28] *The Hako*, pp. 171–172. See also *The Indian in Story and Song*, p. 56.

[29] *Chippewa Music*, I, p. 126, No. 112: "Song of the Trees."

but he was always given the credit of its composition.[30]

The rhythm of this song is peculiarly energizing, and when once established would undoubtedly have a beneficial physical effect. The surprising feature of this case, however, is that the song is said to have been composed and the rhythm created by the sick man himself.[31]

There are many instances of individual artistry among the Australians: —

" The makers of Australian songs, or of the combined songs and dances, are the poets, or bards, of the tribe, and are held in great esteem. Their names are known in the neighboring tribes, and their songs are carried from tribe to tribe, until the very meaning of the words is lost, as well as the original source of the song. It is hard to say how far and how long such a song may travel in the course of time over the Australian continent." [32]

It is interesting to note that many Indian songs are composed by women. The following are instances:

. . . They [the women] would gather in groups at the lodge of the Leader of the war party, and in the hearing of his family would sing a We'-ton song, which should carry straight to the far-away warriors and help them to win the battle . . . The

[30] *Ibid.*, p. 135, No. 121: " I am afraid of the Owl."

[31] *Ibid.*, p. 95, No. 79: " Healing Song." Compare also Franz Boas on *The Central Eskimo,* Report *Bureau of Ethnology,* 1884–1885, p. 649: " Besides these old songs and tales there are a great number of new ones, and, indeed, almost every man has his own tune and his own song. A few of these become great favorites among the Eskimo and are sung like our popular songs."

[32] A. W. Howitt, *The Native Tribes of South-East Australia,* London (1904), p. 414. See also Kurburu's song, composed and sung by a bard called Kurburu, p. 420. Howitt refers to one man who composed when tossing about on the waves in a boat — not a very " communal " method of composition. For other instances of individual composition see George Brown, *Melanesians and Polynesians* (1910), p. 423, C. G. Seligman, *The Melanesians of British New Guinea* (1910), pp. 152, 153, etc.

We'-ton song here given was composed by a Dakota woman.[33]

It is said that the following [Chippewa] song was composed and sung on the field of battle by a woman named Omiskwa'-wegijigo'kwe ("woman of the red sky."), the wife of the leader, who went with him into the fight singing, dancing, and urging him on. At last she saw him kill a Sioux. Full of the fire of battle, she longed to play a man's part and scalp the slain. Custom forbade that Chippewa women use the scalping knife, although they carried the scalps in the victory dance.

Song
at that time
if I had been a man
truly
a man
I would have seized.[34]

Odjib'we [a Chippewa] stated that his wife's brother was killed by the Sioux and that he organized a war party in return. The purpose of the expedition was to attack a certain Sioux village located on an island in Sauk river, but before reaching the village, the Chippewa met a war party of Sioux, which they pursued, killing one man. There were nine Chippewa in Odjib'we's party; not one was killed. They returned home at once and Odjib'we presented the Sioux scalp to his wife Dekum ("across") who held it aloft in the victory dance as she sung the following song.

Odjib'we
our brother
brings back.[35]

[33] Fletcher, *Indian Story and Song*, Weton Song, pp. 81, 85.

So also in the Omaha tribe: "We'tonwaan is an old and untranslatable word used to designate a class of songs composed by women and sung exclusively by them."— Fletcher and LaFlesche, *The Omaha Tribe*, 27th Report, *Bureau of American Ethnology*, p. 421; cf. pp. 320–323 for other types of women's songs.

[34] *Chippewa Music*, II, p. 111, No. 31: "If I Had Been a Man."

[35] *Ibid.*, p. 121, No. 39: Song of Dékum. Several other songs composed by Dekum are given.

Thomas Whiffen quotes a song made by a Boro chief-
tain's daughter, a complaint of her treatment by her own
tribe, having the iterative lines —

> The chief's daughter was lost in the bush
> And no one came to find the spoor.[36]

Much farther evidence of the composition of songs by
women might be cited.[37]

Excellent testimony on the questions of individual com-
position, the refrain, and the relation of the composer to
the chorus comes from the Andamese.[38] " When an An-
damese wishes to make a new song he waits till he feels
inspired to do so, and will then, when alone and engaged
on some occupation, sing to himself till he has hit on a

[36] *The North-West Amazons* (1915), p. 197.

[37] Compare Franz Boas, *Chinook Lays*, p. 224, *Journal of American
Folk-Lore*, 1888: " The greater part of those I have collected were
composed by women." He adds that for a greater number of tunes
the " text is only a meaningless burden." For songs of the Kiowa
composed by a woman, see J. W. Mooney, *The Ghost-Dance Religion*,
14 Report, *Bureau of Ethnology*, Part II, 1896, pp. 1083, 1085, etc.
See also an article of interest by Alexander F. Chamberlain, *Primi-
tive Woman as Poet*, *Journal of American Folk-Lore*, vol. XVI
(1903), pp. 207 ff.; Bücher, *Arbeit und Rhythmus* (1899), ch. viii,
p. 339, " Frauenarbeit und Frauendichtung "; J. C. Andersen, *Maori
Life in Ao-Tea* (1907), p. 500.

R. H. Codrington writes of the Melanesians (*The Melanesians:
Studies in Their Anthropology and Folk-Lore*, Oxford, 1891, p.
334): " A poet or poetess more or less distinguished is probably
found in every considerable village throughout the islands; when
some remarkable event occurs, the launching of a canoe, a visit of
strangers, or a feast, song-makers are engaged to celebrate it and
rewarded," etc.

[38] Pointed out by Professor F. N. Scott, *Modern Language Notes*,
April 1918. See M. V. Porter, *Notes on the Language of the South
Andaman Group of Tribes*, Calcutta (1898), p. 67.

solo and refrain which takes his fancy, and then improves
it to his taste.   His composition would ordinarily refer to
some recent occurrence by which he had been affected,"
" At a dance the soloist stands at the dancing-board and
(often in a falsetto voice) sings his solo and the refrain.
(If he has sung the solo in falsetto, his voice will drop
an octave at the refrain).   If the chorus grasp the re-
frain at once, they sing it; if they do not grasp it, the solo-
ist will repeat it two or three times till the chorus is able
to take it up."   "The solo is sung amid general silence,
and the dance commences with the refrain, being also
accompanied by a clapping of hands and thighs, and the
stamping of the soloist's foot on the sounding board."

The preceding are specimen testimonies.   They might
be added to indefinitely from many sources.   In accounts
of African, Australian, or South American tribes, as well
as of the North American Indians, one comes invariably
upon the instance of the individual who makes a song —
very often in solitude — and the song is recognized as
his.   The great mass of primitive songs sung in com-
munal or other gatherings are either portions of religious
rituals, didactic, or, still oftener, magical in nature.   Far
from being improvised for the occasion, they are sedu-
lously repeated *verbatim,* the least deviation from the rote
form being the occasion, not infrequently, of an entire
recommencement of the ceremony.   Ramon Pane gives the
following testimony concerning the Haytians: [39]   " They
have all the superstitions reduced into old songs, and are
directed by them, as the Moors by the Alcoran.   When
they sing these, they play on an instrument made of wood.
. . . To that music they sing those songs they have got

[39] In Ferdinand Columbus's *Life of Christopher Columbus,* ch. 14.

by heart. The chief men play on it who learn it from
their infancy, and so sing it according to their custom."
Substantially the same account is given by Peter Martyr
d'Anghrera: [40] "When the Spanish asked whoever had
infected them with this mass of ridiculous beliefs, the
natives replied that they received them from their an-
cestors, and that they had been preserved from time im-
memorial in poems which only the sons of chiefs were al-
lowed to learn. These poems are learned by heart, for they
have no writing, and on feast days the sons of chiefs sing
them to the people in the form of sacred chants." Thomas
Whiffen, writing of the Amazonians,[41] speaks of " the
traditional songs of the tribes which are sacred and un-
changeable." " They are the songs that their fathers sang,
and one can find no evidence of the amendation or emenda-
tion of the score on the part of their descendants." " The
dance, like the tobacco palaver, is a dominant factor in
tribal life. For it the Amazonian treasures the songs of
his fathers, and will master strange rhymes and words that
for him no longer have meaning; he only knows that they

[40] *De Orbe Novo*, English trans. by MacNutt, New York (1912),
vol. I, p. 172.

For the North American Indians, see, for example, Washington
Matthews, *Navaho Legends, Memoirs of the American Folk-Lore
Society*, 1897. An account of Navaho traditional songs is given
pp. 23–27. See also note 273, p. 254, *Navaho Music*, by Prof. J. C.
Fillmore. Miss Fletcher gives similar testimony concerning Indian
traditional lays.

[41] *The North-West Amazons* (1915), pp. 208, 190. See also The-
odor Koch-Grünberg, *Zwei Jahre unter den Indianern: Reisen in
Nordwest Brasilien, 1903–1905*. 2 vols., Berlin, 1910. " Die Texte
die dem Aruak und dem Kobéua angehören sind offenbar uralt und
waren von den Sängern teilweise selbst nicht mehr zu deuten,"
vol. II, p. 131.

are the correct lines, the phrases he ought to sing at such functions, because they have always been sung, they are the words of the time-honored tribal melodies."

Songs composed and sung by individuals and songs sung by groups of singers (or "throngs," if you prefer) are to be found in the most primitive of living tribes. That in the earliest stage there was group utterance only, arising from the folk-dance, is fanciful hypothesis. That primitive song is of group composition or collaboration, not individual composition, is quite as fanciful. Again, as far back as we can go in the genesis of song-craft, there are impromptu songs, the spontaneous utterance of present emotion, and there are traditional songs, survivals or revivals of the songs of the past.[42] Among primitive peoples there is no such indissoluble connection between singing and dancing as the italicized observations of Dr. Ehrenreich are supposed to imply. Neither dancing nor song is invariably "choric" in savage any more than in civilized society. Solo dancing, for example, has been reported among the Semang of Perak, the Kwai, and the Andamanese, as well as among the American Indians and numerous other peoples. Koch-Grünberg mentions a dance among tribes north of the Japura where the men and the women dance together in pairs. As for solo singing, the citations given speak for themselves.[43] Even when the

[42] Improvisation exists among the Obongo, Australian, Fijiian, Andamanese, Zulu, Botocudo, and Eskimo tribes, as well as among the North American Indians. For an example of song and dance improvisation constituting a sort of game, see Whiffen, *The North-West Amazons*, p. 208. Traditional songs persist among the Kwai, Australian, Andamanese, Rock Vedda, Semang, Fijiian, Fuegian, Brazilian, and Eskimo tribes, as well as among the North American Indians.

[43] See also citations in note 49.

singing is choral, it is by no means always dance-song, nor accompanied by dancing.   The Kaffirs are said to be fond of singing lustily together, but, if we may trust the observation, " a Kaffir differs from an European vocalist in this point, namely, that he always, if possible, *sits down* when he sings." [44]   Surely these recumbent Kaffirs deserve italics as much as Dr. Ehrenreich's Botocudos.[45]

[44] J. E. Wood, *Uncivilized Races of the World* (Amer. ed., Hartford, 1870), p. 208.

[45] We really know very little concerning the songs of the Botocudos. Dr. Ehrenreich's section dealing with them is very short, and he is chiefly interested in other things than song. These are the specimens he cites: — Gesang beim Tanz. Chor: " Weib jung, stehlen nichts." Ein Weib singt: " Ich, ich will nicht (stehlen)." " Der Häuptling hat keine Furcht "— *Zeitschrift für Ethnologie*, vol. XIX, pp. 33, 61.

Testimony concerning the songs of other Brazilian tribes may be found in J. B. Steere's *Narrative of a Visit to the Indian Tribes of the Purus River, Annual Report* of the Smithsonian Institution, 1901, pp. 363–393. The following are songs of the Hypurinás (cannibals), and are individualistic in character: " The leaf that calls my lover when tied in my girdle " (Indian girl's song) ; " I have my arrows ready and wish to kill you "; " Now no one can say I am not a warrior. I return victorious from the battle "; " I go to die, my enemy shall eat me."

The following are some songs of the Paumari, a " humble cowardly people who live in deadly fear of the Hypurinás "; " My mother when I was little carried me with a strap on her back. But now I am a man I don't need my mother any more "; " The Toucan eats fruit in the edge of my garden, and after he eats he sings "; " The jaguar fought with me, and I am weary, I am weary." The following they call the song of the turtle: " I wander, always wander, and when I get where I want to go, I shall not stop, but still go on."

Hunting songs of the Bakairí, of the Xingu river region, egoistic in character, are cited by Dr. Max Schmidt, *Indianerstudien in Zentralbrasilien*, Berlin, 1905, pp. 421–424.

The " I " of these songs of South American tribes cannot always

The conception of individual song can be shown to exist among the very lowest peoples. Professor Gummere's belief is that human beings get together for rhythmic movement, begin to sing, and thus song is born. But the same savage tribes that sing in groups tell stories in which individual songs appear. Among the myths of the wilder tribes of Eastern Brazil,[46] for example, there are many in which the composition and singing of songs by individuals form important incidents. This fact shows plainly that the authors of these myths were perfectly familiar with the conception of individual composition. Granting the manifestations of primitive singing and dancing throngs which seem so decisive to many scholars, they are capable of quite other interpretations than those which are usually assigned them.

III — THE " BALLAD " AS THE EARLIEST POETIC FORM

And now what truth is in the assumption that the ballad-dance is the germ from which emerged the three separate arts, poetry, music, dance? A passage by Professor Moulton, affirming this, has been cited, and this passage presents without doubt, a view now widely accepted. The opinion is prevalent among folk-lorists and students of literature that since ballads come down to us by tradition, they represent poetry in its most primitive form.

be "racial." The context shows that, sometimes, at least, it must be egoistic, as in the individualistic songs of the North American Indians, or in the solo songs of men or women with grievances among the Brazilian cannibals. See Whiffen, *The North-West Amazons*, pp. 196, 197, etc.

[46] Illustrated in *O Selvagem*, the well-known collection of José V. Couto de Magalhães.

We are told that ballads can best be studied by studying the poetry of races least civilized.[47]

Let us ask, first, in what sense the word " ballad " is used by those who derive poetry from it. Does Professor Moulton, for example, use the word ballad in its etymological sense of " dance song," leaving undetermined the character of the words, whether meaningless vocables, purely lyrical, or prevailingly narrative? Usually the classification " ballad " is employed of lyric verses having a narrative element. By " ballad " we are supposed to mean a narrative song, a story in verse, a short narrative told lyrically. It is a loose usage which permits scholars to use the word in the sense both of dance song and of lyrical narrative, in the same work; the ambiguity is unnecessary.[48] If ballad means something like dance song, or choral dance, or folk-dance accompanied by improvisation and refrain, the term ballad-dance is tautological; for all ballads involve dancing. One wishes for more precision. But this need not detain us here.

[47] Professor W. H. Hudson, for example, in *An Introduction to the Study of Literature* (1911), p. 138, speaks of the ballads as " poetry of primitive models." He refers to the ballad, p. 136, as representing " one of the earliest stages in the evolution of the poetic art." So Professor W. M. Hart, *English Popular Ballads* (1916), p. 51, " Ballads are the one great and significant survival of . . . early universal poetry." Professor Gummere assures us (*Old English Ballads*, p. lxxxiv) that " the so-called narrative lyric, or ballad in stricter sense, was the universal form of poetry of the people."

[48] In which sense, for example, does Professor G. P. Krapp (*The Rise of English Literary Prose*, 1915, Preface) use "ballad" when he writes, " Poetry of primitive origins, for example, the ballad, often attains a finality of form which art cannot better, but not so with prose"?

In whichever sense the term ballad be used, it is some-
what rash to place the ballad dance so certainly at the
source of man's musical and poetical expression. We have
just seen that there is individual composition and singing,
song unaccompanied by dancing, and dance unaccom-
panied by song, as far down in the cultural scale as we
can go. Certainly if ballad means, as usually it does,
song-story, the ballad was *not* the earliest form of poetry;
and primitive people *never* danced to ballads. The earli-
est songs we can get track of are purely lyrical, not
narrative. The melody is the important thing; the words,
few in number and sometimes meaningless, are relatively
negligible. Moreover, these songs are on many themes, or
have many impulses beside festal dances. There are heal-
ers' songs, conjurers' songs, hunting songs, game-songs,
love songs, hymns, prayers, complaints or laments, vic-
tory songs, satires, songs of women and children, and lyrics
of personal feeling and appeal. The lullaby is an old
lyric form. Who cares to affirm that lullabies were un-
known to our aboriginal ancestors? Yet the lullaby has
nothing to do with the singing and dancing throng. Nor
has that other very early species, the medicine man or
healer's solos; nor have gambling or game songs,[49] or

[49] See Stewart Culin, *Games of the North American Indian*, 24
Report, *Bureau of Ethnology* (1907), for an account of singing
in the Moccasin or Hidden-Ball game, pp. 335 ff. Mention is made
of solo singing among the Chippewa, the Menominee, the Miami,
the Seneca, the Wyandot. See also Edward Sapir, *Song Recitative
in Paiute Mythology, Journal of American Folk-Lore* (1910), p.
455, vol. XXIII: "Generally Indian music is of greatest significance
when combined with the dance in ritualistic or ceremonial perform-
ances. Nevertheless the importance of music in non-ceremonial
acts . . . should not be minimized."

love songs.[50]   Primitive labor songs are social, but they
do not involve dancing, though some may have a certain
relation to it, and they are not ballads. The class that
is nearest the real ballad, in that it is based on happenings,
or on the composer's experiences, is not by any means
the largest or the most important group for primitive
song. Songs of this latter type may be suggested by some
event, or may present some situation; but they tell no
story in the sense of real telling. That demands length,
elaboration, completeness, beyond primitive powers. If
we try to fix chronology, it is most plausible to begin with
rhythmic action and with melody. Professor Gummere
thinks that melody is born of rhythmic action. But vocal
action of the singing type, i. e., melody, may well be
as instinctive in man as in birds. Action and melody
in singing may well have come together; for song inter-

There are solo-singing Bantu, Zulu, Fuegian, etc., witch-doctors
and medicine men, as well as solo-singing North American Indian
medicine men and gamesters. See also, for instances of solo
singing, H. A. Junod, *Les Chantes et les Contes des Ba-Ronga*,
Lausanne, 1897; also G. Landtman, *The Poetry of the Kiwai
Papuans, Folk-Lore*, vol. XXIV (1913); Howitt, *The Native Tribes
of South-East Australia;* James Cowan, *The Maoris of New Zea-
land;* E. H. Gomes, *Seventeen Years Among the Sea Dyaks of Borneo*,
as "The song of mourning is among some tribes sung by a profes-
sional wailer, generally a woman."

[50] According to Whiffen, love songs, sacred songs, and nursery
songs do not exist among the Boros, *The North-West Amazons*
(1915), p. 208. But they are known among other tribes, though
they play no conspicuous rôle, from the nature of things. See the
references for primitive love songs and childhood songs in Mackenzie,
The Evolution of Literature, pp. 140, 144, etc. They are known
among the North-American Indians. See Frances Densmore, *Teton
Sioux Music*, pp. 370 ff., 509, 492, 493 (lullaby); also many other
writers on Indian song.

prets primarily feeling, emotion, not motion. In any case, words came later than melody, and real narrative later yet. As a lyrical species, the narrative song is a late, not an early, poetical development. If we look at what certain evidence we have, primitive songs are very brief, the words are less important than the music, indeed they need hardly be present; and they rarely tell a story. No instances are known to me in which a primitive song tells a story with real elaboration or completeness. Nor need these songlets always have their origin in the choral — specifically in the improvisation and communal elaboration of a festal dance. Why, then, apply the term *ballad* to the brief and simple lyrical utterances, often nothing more than the repetition of a few syllables, or of one syllable, which — according to the evidence — make up the great body of primitive song?

But it is time to bring up a few illustrations.

First place may well be given to the words of Miss Alice Fletcher, who has had thirty-five years of acquaintance with Indian music:

The word "song" to our ears, suggests words arranged in metrical form and adapted to be "set to music," as we say. The native word which is translated "song" does not suggest any use of words. To the Indian, the music is of primal importance, words may or may not accompany the music. When words are used in a song, they are rarely employed as in a narrative, the sentences are not apt to be complete. In songs belonging to a religious ceremony the words are few and partake of a mnemonic character. They may refer to some symbol, may suggest the conception or the teaching the symbol stands for, rarely more than that. Vocables are frequently added to the word or words to eke out the musical measure. It sometimes happens that a song has no words at all, only vocables are used to float the voice. Whether vocables alone are used or used in connection with words, they are never a random collection of syllables. An examination of hundreds of songs shows that the vocables used fall into classes; one class is used for songs denoting action, another class for songs of a contemplative character, and it is also noted that when once vocables are adapted to a song they are never changed but are treated as if they were actual words.[51]

She writes elsewhere to the same effect:

In Indian song and story we come upon a time when poetry is not yet differentiated from story and story not yet set free from song. We note that the song clasps the story as part of its being, and the story itself is not fully told without the cadence of the song. . . . The difference between spontaneous Indian melodies and the compositions of modern masters would seem to be not one of kind but of degree. . . . Many Indian songs have no words at all, vocables only being used to float the voice.[52]

The investigator of Ojibway song also finds the melody to be more important than the words, and has nothing to say of an inevitable relation between dancing and song.[53]

His [the Ojibway] poetry is not only inseparable but indistinguishable from music. . . . Among all civilized peoples the art of expression through verse is one thing, and the art of expression through modulated tones is quite another, linked though they often are by the deliberate intent of the composer, and always associated in the popular mind; in the Ojibway conception the two arts are not merely linked inseparably, they are fused in one. . . .

The Ojibway is more gifted in music than in poetry; he has wrought out a type of beautiful melody, much of it perfect in form; his verse, for the most part, has not emerged from the condition of raw material.

[51] *The Study of Indian Music*, 1915, pp. 231–232.
[52] *Indian Story and Song*, pp. 121, 124, 125.
[53] Burton, *American Primitive Music*, pp. 106, 172, 173.

He does sing his new melody to meaningless syllables, tentatively correcting it here and there, but meantime experimenting with words that convey meaning; and the probability is that the precise sentiment of the words finally accepted is established by rhythmic considerations, those that fall readily into the scheme of accents appealing to him as the most suitable vehicle for the melody.

The melody and the idea are the essential parts of a Midé song. Sometimes only one or two words occur in a song. . . . Many of the words used in a Midé song are unknown in the conversational Chippewa of the present time.[54]

A number of Chippewa songs, as transcribed, have no words. Some of these songs originally may have had words and in a limited number of love songs the words partake so much of the nature of a soliloquy that they cannot conveniently be translated and given with the music. The words of most of the Chippewa songs are few in number and suggest rather than express the idea of the song. Only in the love songs and in few of the Midé songs are the words continuous.

Many tribes other than the North American Indians appear to have songs which they can no longer interpret. The survival in song of words the meaning of which is lost is world-wide. We are told of the savage tribes of New Guinea that " Most of the songs are without words or with words the meaning of which is lost." [55] Koch-Grünberg says that there are old dances among the Tukano with words no longer understood." [56] The same testimony is

---

[54] Frances Densmore, *Chippewa Music*, I (1910), pp. 14, 15, and II (1913.), p. 2. Similarly Washington Matthews, *Journal of American Folk-Lore*, 1894, p. 185, writes of traditional songs among the Navahos, "One song consists almost exclusively of meaningless or archaic vocables. Yet not one syllable may be forgotten or misplaced."

[55] Henry Newton, *In Far New Guinea* (1914), p. 147.

[56] *Zwei Jahre unter den Indianern*, etc. (1910), vol. II, p. 254.

made concerning the Naga tribes, the Australian natives, the Zulu, and Brazilian tribes.[57]

Such evidence may be multiplied indefinitely. The brevity of Indian songs is striking. Many have few words, some one word, and some no words. The songs of other savage peoples show the same characteristic. There are one-word traditional poems among the African Kwai, and two-word traditional poems of the Botocudos and the Eskimos. These are not narrative songs, and they need not be dance songs; for savage peoples do not always dance their verses. They are not, then, "ballads." Nor need they have any relation to choral improvisation.

Literary historians have dwelt too much, it seems to me, on the festal throng and communal improvisation and the folk-dance, when dealing with the "beginnings of poetry," until the whole subject has been thrown out of focus. The term ballad might well be left out of account altogether and reserved for the lyric species, appearing late in literary history, the "epic in little," or "short narrative told lyrically" exemplified in the conventional ballad collections. If we are to mean by ballads narrative songs like those of the middle ages, or narrative songs wherever they appear, we should certainly cease placing the ballad at the source of primitive poetry. The conception of a ballad as something improvised more or less spontaneously by a dancing throng should be given up. Even savage peoples do not compose characteristically in that way. And even among savage peoples, the pres-

[57] T. Hodson, *The Naga Tribes of Manipur* (1911), p. 68; B. Spencer and F. J. Gillen, *The Native Tribes of Central Australia* (1899), p. 281; H. Callaway, *Religious Systems of the Amazulu,* etc. (1870); Whiffen, *The North-West Amazons,* pp. 190, 208.

ence of refrains need not "point straight to the singing
and dancing throng." It is not proved that the ballad,
in any sense, came first, or even that choral songs pre-
ceded solos. It is likely enough that choral songs and
solos co-existed from the beginning, or even that solos
preceded, for all that can be certainly known. The as-
sumption that group power to sing, to compose songs, and
to dance, precedes individual power to do these things,[58]
is fatuously speculative. It rests neither on " overwhelm-
ing evidence " nor on probability. The individual ought
to be able to engage in rhythmic motion, to compose tunes,
and then to evolve words for these tunes, at least as early
as he is able to do these things along with others of his
kind. And let it be said again that it is safer to affirm
that the primitive lyric, whether individual or choral, is not
the ballad but the song — more strictly, the songlet.

[58] Erich Schmidt ("Anfänge der Literatur," p. 9, in *Kultur der
Gegenwart*, Leipzig, 1906, i) writes: . . . schon weil keine Masse
nur den einfachsten Satz unisona improvisieren kann und alle
romantischen Schwärmereien von der urheberlos singenden "Volks-
seele" eitel Dunst sind, muss sich Sondervortag und Massenaus-
bruch sehr früh gliedern. Einer schreit zuerst, einer singt und
springt zuerst, die Menge macht es ihm nach, entweder treulich
oder indem sie bei unartikulierten Refrains, bei einzelnen Worten,
bei wiederkehrenden Sätzen beharrt.

In this connection, since it deserves to be cited somewhere, may
be quoted a passage from von Humboldt: "The Indians pretend
that when the araguatos [howling monkeys] fill the forests with
their howling, there is always one that chants as leader of the
chorus."— A. von Humboldt, *Travels in the Equinoctial Regions of
America*, Bohn edition, vol. ii, p. 70.

CHAPTER II

THE MEDIÆVAL BALLAD AND THE DANCE

If the ballad, whether defined as dance song or as narrative lyric, is not the archetypal poetic form, preserving the model of primitive song, if it did not originate, more specifically than other lyric verse, in the festal dance songs of primitive peoples, is it not, at least, to be associated with the dances or the dance songs of the Middle Ages? Such association is customary. The primary definition of the English ballad, in English dictionaries of the nineteenth century, is "dance song." The etymology of the name makes linkage of the ballad with the dances of mediæval times practically inevitable. A few quotations will make clear the present state of opinion.

The leading American writer on ballads in recent times, Professor F. J. Gummere, affirmed, "But there is neither hurry nor compact narrative in the real ballad, so named not because it was sung at a dance but because it was a dance, a dramatic situation, unchanged in bulk and plan, but shifting its parts in tune with these until a climax is attained." [1] According to Professor G. L. Kittredge, "It appears that there is no lack of characteristic traits . . . which justify the conjecture that the history of balladry, if we could follow it back in a straight line without interruptions would lead us to a very simple condition of

---

[1] *Democracy and Poetry* (1911), p. 191.

society, to the singing and dancing throng, to a period of communal composition." [2]   Professor Henry Beers wrote, " It should never be forgotten that the ballad . . . was not originally a written poem but a song and dance." [3]   More qualification characterizes the words of Professor Charles S. Baldwin, " They [the ballads] may have been originally dance songs with communal refrain."   " Bride-stealing, a situation often told in ballads, may in some far off day have been half presented, half represented by a dancing chorus and villagers, singing one detail after another and iterating a common refrain." [4]

To pass from American opinion to British, that excellent ballad scholar, Professor W. P. Ker, writes, " The proper form of the ballads is the same as the *carole*, with narrative substance added.   Anything will do for a ring dance, either at a wake in a churchyard or in a garden. . . . At first a love song was the favorite sort, with a refrain of *douce amie*, and so on. . . . The narrative ballad was most in favor where people were fondest of dancing.   The love-song or the nonsense verses could not be kept up so long; something more was wanted, and this was given by the story; also as the story was always dramatic, more or less, with different people speaking, the entertainment was all the better."   " The old Teutonic narrative poetry may have grown out of a very old ballad custom, where the narrative element increased and grad-

[2] Kittredge and Sargent, *English and Scottish Popular Ballads* (1904), Introd. p. xxii.

[3] *English Romanticism in the XVIII Century* (1898), p. 270. Professor Beers's discussion, in this volume, of the English and Scottish ballads, their content and special qualities, is very suggestive and stimulating.

[4] *English Mediæval Literature* (1914), pp. 237, 242.

ually killed the lyric, so that recitation of a story by a minstrel took the place of the dancing chorus." In the following passage he suggests a specific development: —

> Probably the old ballad chorus in its proper dancing form was going out of use in England about 1400. Barbour, a contemporary of Chaucer, speaks of girls singing "ballads" "at their play"; Thomas Deloney in the time of Elizabeth describes the singing of a ballad refrain; and the game lives happily still, in songs of *London Bridge* and others. But it becomes more and more common for ballads to be sung or recited to an audience sitting still; ballads were given out by minstrels, like the minstrel of *Chevy Chase*. Sometimes ballads are found swelling into something like a narrative poem; such is the famous ballad of *Adam Bell, Clim o' the Clough, and William of Cloudeslee*.[5]

W. T. Young summarizes as follows: "Scholars are coming to the conclusion that they [the ballads] originated, as their refrains seem to indicate, in a song accompanied by dancing and a chorus, not unlike the French *carole*." [6] Mr. T. F. Henderson, a keen and sane ballad scholar, like Professor Ker, cannot concede that the ballad had its origin in individual peasant improvisation nor that it was

[5] *English Literature: Mediæval* (1912). Home University Library edition, pp. 159, 161, 164. It is difficult to concede that Barbour's "ballads" (probably *ballades* or love songs) give evidence bearing on the lyric-epic type now known as the traditional ballad. And if the Deloney "ballad refrain" survives in games and songs, not in ballads, it would seem to reinforce the inference (see pp. 55, 65) that mediæval dance songs in England and mediæval lyric-epics or ballads proper were not the same species, therefore not of identical origin. Support is lent, not to the theory that the earlier dance songs developed into ballads of the Child type, but to the inference that the two were distinct in origin and destiny.

[6] *Introduction to the Study of English Literature* (1914). Based on, and an introduction to *The Cambridge History of English Literature*.

the creation of rural dancing throngs, but he admits that
it might have borne some relation to dancing of more
aristocratic type. " This kind of ballad [the serious
lyric-epic] for its full effectiveness as a song or recital
called in originally the aid of a chorus, and, probably, of
the dance," ". . . it often added to the emotional impres-
sion by the device of the refrain sung by a chorus, and at
one time probably danced as well as sung." Elsewhere
he speaks of " The earlier ballads sung probably to the
dance, or at least made to be sung with choral effect." [7]

In the following pages it is proposed to canvass the evi-
dence for the definition of ballads as dance songs, or
rather for the assumption of dance-song origin for ballads,
and to make inquiry as to its validity. Particular refer-
ence is had to the English and Scottish ballad type.

I — THE NAME " BALLAD "

Much of the confusion in scholarly and literary discus-
sion of the English and Scottish ballads and their Ameri-
can descendants or analogues, rests on ambiguous and
contradictory usages of the word " ballad." It has been
employed for as many lyric types as were " sonnet " and
" ode," and it has hardly yet settled down into consistent
application. The popular use of the word for a short
song, often sentimental in character, or for the music for
such a song, is clear enough; but its most recently de-
veloped meaning of narrative song, currently employed by
literary historians, is only now assuming initial place in
the dictionaries.[8] It is this newly developed usage which

[7] *The Ballad in Literature* (1912), pp. 6, 8, 87, 95.
[8] Although the meaning narrative song gained headway in the

has brought confusion. For though the shifts in meaning of the term " ballad " have often been noted and traced, clarity or consistency in its employment have not followed, even among the tracers. They distinguish what they mean by ballad clearly enough; but they lose sight of their own distinctions when they come to theorizing about their material. Within the last one hundred and fifty years the name has been restricted, among specialists, to a type of English song to which it did not belong originally, and a type which is not called by that name in other languages, save when the usage has been carried over from the English.[9] The etymology of " ballad " should not be given undue weight, since the attachment of the name to

eighteenth century, it was not very clearly recognized in the *New English Dictionary*, 1888. The entry given fifth place is " A simple spirited poem in short stanzas, originally a ' ballad ' in sense 3 [popular songs — often broadsides] in which some popular story is graphically narrated. (This sense is essentially modern.)" *The New Webster International*, 1910, also gives this meaning fifth place, but contributes clarity: " A popular kind of short narrative poem adapted for singing; especially a romantic poem of the kind characterized by simplicity of structure and impersonality of authorship." In *The Standard Dictionary*, 1917, is entered as the first meaning of the word: " A simple lyrical poem telling a story or legend, usually of popular origin; as the ballad of Chevy Chase." Here the older order of definition is reversed, recognizing the change established long before in usage.

[9] The Danish name for pieces of the English ballad type is *folke-viser*. The Spanish name is *romances*. The German usage of *Ballade* follows the English; German poets derived much of their balladry from England. The name is applied to short poems in which the narrative element is as important as the lyrical. See F. A. Brockhaus, *Konversations-Lexicon*, Berlin and Vienna, 1894. Pieces of the English lyric-epic type have no specific name in French. They are grouped under the large class of *chansons populaires*, a name as inclusive as our " folk-song." But see also note 13.

the material which it describes is recent. Over-emphasis upon its etymology, and the double and triple senses in which contemporary scholars use the term, have puzzled and misled many earnest students. Writers who insist that they have clearly in mind what they mean sometimes apply the name " ballad " to dance songs, sometimes to narrative songs, sometimes to pure lyrics, and sometimes to all three.

Ballad is derived from *ballare,* to dance, and historically it means dancing song; it is associated etymologically with *ballet,* a form of dance. In the Romance languages, from which the word issued into general European currency, it came to apply to various types of lyrics. The French and Italian pieces taking the name, or various forms of it, are genuinely lyrical; they are to be associated with dance origins, and they do not narrate happenings or suggest action. Many were used, it is certain, as dance songs.[10] To be a folk-ballad, not merely a folk-song, an English piece must tell a story. Poems of the type of Rossetti's *Sister Helen* or *Stratton Water,* or Longfellow's *The Wreck of the Hesperus,* are termed " literary " ballads, as over against anonymous traditional ballads, like *Sir Patrick Spens.* The name ballad, meaning primarily, as we have seen, a dance-lyric is not entirely satisfactory for these lyric-epics. It gained its distinctive application by chance rather than by historic right, and it gained this application late. Owing partly to the etymology of the name, partly to the hypotheses of certain critics, who associate the origin of the English and Scottish pieces with the choral dances of mediæval festal communes, ballads

---

[10] Dante, for example, assigns *ballata* a lower plane than song proper or sonnet on account of its dependence on the aid of dancers.

of the type collected by Professor F. J. Child have come to be associated with the dance to a degree which the evidence does not justify. The dance is given place in the foreground, as essential in defining the type and its origin, instead of being made something remote and subsidiary. For the Child pieces, the etymology of the name should be given little or no emphasis; insistence on it is likely to be misleading. In fact, dance-genesis has more immediate connection with English lyrics of many other types, in the consideration of which we are not asked to have it constantly before us, than it has with the English ballads; for instance, with the *ballade,* or the *rondeau.*

The name " ballad " was not applied specifically to heroic or romantic narrative songs until the eighteenth century. Thomas Deloney, in the age of Elizabeth, referred to *The Fair Flower of Northumberland* and to *Flodden Field* as " songs." Sidney speaks of the " old song " of *The Percy and the Douglas.* Pepys uses the same term for narrative songs. Philip's *New World of English Words* [11] defines " ballad " as " a Common Song sung up and down the streets." In Dr. Johnson's *Dictionary* " ballad " means " song " and nothing more. It was Ritson who first stated the distinction that now obtains. " With us, songs of sentiment, expression, or even description, are properly called songs, in contradistinction to mere narrative pieces, which we now denominate ballads." [12] For several centuries earlier the name had been applied

[11] Sixth edition, 1705.

[12] Introduction to his *Select Collection of English Songs,* 3 vols., 2nd edition, 1813. Shenstone and Michael Bruce had expressed the distinction earlier (see S. B. Hustvedt, *Ballad Criticism in Scandinavia and Great Britain,* 1916, p. 254), but it was first publicly enunciated by Ritson.

with miscellaneous reference. It might be given to a short didactic poem, a love poem (as sometimes now), to poems of satire and vituperation, to political pieces, to hymns and religious pieces, to elegiac pieces, occasionally to narrative pieces; in short, to lyrics of any type. Thus its specific application to verse of the Child type came late and not by inheritance, but arbitrarily. Nor did the etymology of the name play any part in the selection of it for the pieces to which it was applied.

It will be sufficient to sketch in summary here the stages of development for English in the usage of the name ballad.[13]

When Chaucer uses the term ballad it is for lyrics of the fixed type imported from the French, the *Balade de Bon Conseyl,* or *Lak of Stedfastnesse,* or the *Compleynt to His Empty Purse,* not to lyric-epics.[14] Ballad was long used of dance songs of various types, as a few

[13] The entries in *The New English Dictionary* have been referred to. Fourteen pages of matter illustrative of the history of *ballade* are given in Larousse's *Grand Dictionnaire Universel du* XIX *Siècle,* Paris (1867), ranging from the first entry "chanson à danser" to, "Aujourd'hui, ode d'un genre familier et le plus souvent légendaire et fantastique: les ballades de Schiller, de Goethe, etc." Nothing is said of a narrative element. But see especially Helen Louise Cohen, *The Ballade,* Columbia University Studies in English and Comparative Literature, New York, 1915. According to Miss Cohen, the word is used in contemporary French in the way in which it has come to be used in English and in German. "In France, at the present time, the same word, *ballade,* serves for the English or Scottish popular ballad and for a certain kind of narrative poem, written in imitation of German authors like Uhland, as well as for the artificially fixed lyric poem." The usages of "ballad" for English have been traced by Professor Gummere, *Old English Ballads,* pp. xviii ff.

[14] An excellent example of his usage is found in the Prologue to

citations will show; e. g., these lines from Dunbar's *Golden Targe,* of about 1500:

> And sang ballettes with mighty notes clere,
> Ladyes to daunce full sobirly assayit.

Ascham writes in 1545,[15] " these balades and roundes, these galiardes, pauanes and daunces." A passage in George Gascoigne's *Certain Notes of Instruction,* 1575, is very specific. He thinks of the term mainly in Chaucer's sense:

There is also another kinde, called Ballade, and therof are sundrie sortes: for a man may write ballade in a staffe of sixe lines, every line conteyning eighte or sixe sillables, wherof the firste and third, second and fourth do rime acrosse, and the fifth and sixth do rime togither in conclusion. You may write also your *ballad* of tenne syllables, rimying as before is declared, but these two were wont to be most comonly used in *ballade,* whiche propre name was (I thinke) derived of this worde in Italian *Ballare,* whiche signifieth to daunce, and indeed, those kinds of rimes serve beste for daunces and light matters.

Ben Jonson, in *Love Restored,* writes " Unless we should come in like Morrice-dancers and whistle our ballet ourselves." All these citations show loose reference to amatory songs, and dance songs, lyrical, not narrative in character. The word is also applied to pieces of the various types enumerated at the end of the preceding paragraph. Cotgrave's *Dictionary of the French and English Tongues,* 1611, associates the word with dance song. Burton writes,

The Legend of Good Women, where he has his characters dance in a circle " as it were in carole-wise " while they sang the *ballade* —

" Hyd, Absolon, thy gilte tresses clere."

[15] *Toxophilus,* Arber ed., p. 39.

Anatomy of Melancholy, III, 1, i, " Castalio would not have
young men read the Canticles because to his thinking it
was too light and amorous a tract, a ballad of ballads, as
our old English translation hath it." Percy, as often
pointed out, employs ballad in his *Reliques* with miscella-
neous application. Ritson's contribution toward estab-
lishing the word in its latest meaning has been quoted
already. Coleridge's use is modern when he writes of
" The grand old ballad of *Sir Patrick Spens.*" To sum-
marize the stages for English:

1. Ballad in the fourteenth century meant the French
art lyric with fixed form. The name could be given to
a dance song, though the latter was more often called a
carol. Ballad, in the period when it could mean dance
song, did not mean " narrative lyric."

2. In the Elizabethan period, ballads, ballets, ballants,
etc., are terms loosely associated with song, or lyric verse
of various kinds. The name could be applied to dance
songs, among these types and, though infrequently, to
narrative lyrics.

3. In the eighteenth century, ballad continues in loose
popular usage. With specialists it comes to have particu-
lar reference to narrative songs. The narrative songs
which the eighteenth century collected were not dance
songs, and they are not the pieces called by cognate names
in the Romance languages, from which ballad, in lyric
nomenclature, is derived.

4. In the nineteenth century, ballad continues in loose
popular reference as synonymous with song. In the use
of specialists it is increasingly applied to narrative songs;
by the twentieth century, this has become the primary
meaning. The variant *ballade,* in the French and four-

teenth-century English sense, is revived, in the nineteenth century, with the re-introduction of the fixed lyric type.

This sketch should have made clear that a definition of the ballad as " a narrative lyric made and sung at the dance and handed down in popular tradition " is not warranted, for English ballads, by the history of the word. For a valid etymological argument for ballad as a dance song, one would have to derive the lyric-epic species, *ballad,* from the fixed art species, the *ballade.* And there is no sufficient proof that narrative lyrics were ever, anywhere, at any time, by any people, made and sung at the dance. The dance songs of primitive peoples are not narrative, and the earliest English dance songs are not narrative. Nor is this longer definition, also Professor Gummere's,[16] better. " The popular ballad, as it is understood for the purpose of these selections, is a narrative, in lyric form, with no traces of individual authorship, and is preserved mainly by oral tradition. In its earliest stages it was meant to be sung by a crowd, and got its name from the dance to which it furnished the sole musical accompaniment." The first sentences are unimpeachable, but the last is not. The lyric type to which reference is made did not get its name until the late eighteenth century, and then took it by borrowing or transference from songs of another character, for which it was more appropriate. It could not have taken its name from its origin, nor is its name evidence as to its origin.

16 In *The Popular Ballad* (1907), pp. 75, 344, etc., and " Ballads " in Warner's *Library of the World's Best Literature.* " Their very name," we are reminded, " tells of external origin at the communal dance."

II — DANCE SONGS PROPER

The name actually given in England to dance songs of
the Middle Ages was " carol." We hear of carols before
we hear of ballads. There is a familiar picture of a high-
born throng singing to the caroling of a lady in the Chau-
cerian *Romance of the Rose:*

> The folk of which I telle you so,
> Upon a carole wenten tho.

> A lady caroled hem that hyghte,
> Gladness (the) blisful, the lyghte . . .
> > 743–6.

> Tho mightest thou caroles seen,
> And folk (ther) daunce and mery been
> And make many a fair tourning
> Upon the grene gras springing . . .
> > 759–62.

The description is continued, 802–15, 850–54, and on-
wards, and teaches us no little concerning mediæval dance
customs. Other passages, illustrating the use of carol for
dance song, in the next century, might be multiplied.[17]
Many are cited in the dictionaries.

Suppose we try to put ourselves back into the old world

[17] Compare *Gawayn and the Green Knight:* " This King Arthur
lay royally at Camelot at Christmas tide with many fine lords, the
best of men, all the rich brethren of the Round Table, with right
rich revel and careless mirth. There full many heroes tourneyed
betimes, jousted full gaily; then returned these gentle knights to
the court to make carols. For there the feast was held full fifteen
days alike with all the meat and the mirth that men could devise.
Such a merry tumult, glorious to hear; joyful din by day, dancing
at night. All was high joy in hall and chambers with lords and
ladies as pleased them best."

of dance songs. What kind of song was it which the lady sang, and to which the others danced? It might have been a *ballade,* or roundel, or " virelai," or some type of art lyric, with fixed refrain of regular occurrence; for such lyrics were used for dancing.[18] Or it might have had greater suggestion of animation and movement, like many examples afforded by Old French verse; [19] or it might have been a gay love lyric. That it was anything like *King Estmere,* or *Thomas Rymer,* or *Edward,* or *Lord Randal,* is most improbable. And when peasant throngs, as over against aristocrats, danced in feudal times, they did not dance, as I believe, to pieces of the lyric-epic type just mentioned. Nor, as a general thing, the rule rather than the exception, did they dance to their own improvisations. It is more likely that they danced to current inherited songs, appropriate for dance purposes, with, possibly enough, a bygone vogue in higher circles behind them; that is, if we keep the analogies of existent dance songs before us.

The following lines from Gawain Douglas point to the dancing of his characters mostly to lyric and amatory matter: [20]

> Sum sing sangis, dansis ledys and roundis
> With vocis schill, quhill all the dail resoundis
> Quharso thai walk into thar carolyng
> For amorus lays doith the Roches ryng:

[18] See the quotation from Chaucer's Prologue to the *Legend of Good Women,* note 14 preceding.

[19] See the *ballettes,* in Jeanroy's *Les Origines de la Poésie Lyrique en France au Moyen Age;* and his letter, cited in Miss Cohen's *The Ballade,* p. 15; also Joseph Bédier, *Les Plus Anciennes Danses Françaises, Revue des Deux Mondes,* Jan. 15, 1906, p. 398.

[20] *Æneid,* Prologue of Bk. XII.

And sang, 'the schyp salys our the salt faym
Will bryng thir merchandis and my lemman haym';
Sum other syngis, I wil be blyth·and lycht
Mine hart is lent upon so gudly wight.

But we need not speak speculatively of mediæval dance
songs. Many remain to us; and it is possible to derive
from them pretty clear ideas as to what the typical ones
were like. A couplet used for dance purposes remains
from the twelfth century. Ritson [21] cites from Lam-
barde's *Dictionary of England* this anecdote: "In tyme
of Hen. II. [*anno* 1173] Robert therl of Leycester . . .
purposed to spoile the town and thabbey [of St. Edmundes
Burye] . . . Now while his gallauntes paused upon the
heathe, they fell to daunce and singe,

"Hoppe Wylikin, hoppe Wyllykin,
Ingland is thyne and myne, etc."

The well-known *Sumer is icumen in* of the thirteenth
century, might have been a dance song — its animation
and movement would make it appropriate; and welcomes
to spring, when dancing on the green or in the grove could
be resumed, were common for dance-song usage in all parts
of Europe. A classic example of a dance song is that
preserved by Fabyan (1516), celebrating the victory of
the Scots at Bannockburn: [22]

[21] *Dissertation on Ancient Songs and Music* (ed. of 1829), p. xl.
The fragment of the dance song is to be found in Matthew of Paris's
Historia Anglorum sive, ut vulgo dicitur, Historia Minor. Ed. Sir
F. Madden, Rolls series (1866), vol. I, p. 381. See also J. F.
Royster, *English Tags in Matthew of Paris, Modern Language Re-
view*, vol. IV, p. 509.
[22] *Concordance of Histories.*

> Maydens of Englonde, sore may ye morne,
> For your lemmans ye have loste at Bannockisborne!
> With a hewe a lowe.
> What wenyth the Kynge of Englonde
> So soon to have wonne Scotlonde:
> With a rumby lowe.

This song, says Fabyan, " was after many days sung in dances, in caroles of the maidens and minstrels of Scotland." High-born maidens they were, too, most likely, not peasants. It is appropriate for a dance song. It is lyrical, not a verse story. The refrain is important, and holds it together; but it is not narrative. It is nothing like a Child piece, and never became like one, so far as there is evidence.[23]

[23] King Cnut's song is often said (Gummere, *Cambridge History of English Literature*, vol. II, ch. xvii, *The Popular Ballad*, pp. 58 ff, *Old English Ballads*, p. 254) to give us our " first example of actual ballad structure and the ballad's metrical form which is to be met in English records." The beginning of the song and an account of its composition, as the king's boat neared Ely, is given in the *Historia Eliensis* of 1166. But whether the song affords valid illustration of ballad history turns upon whether its missing lines are epic or lyric, i.e., whether it was a ballad or merely a song. There is no proof that it was lyric-epic in character, the presence of rhyme and the strophe structure are both doubtful, and there is no proof that it was a dance song (as Professor Gummere assumed when he persistently translated the chronicler's *in choris publice* as " sung in their dances "), or that it ever came to be used as such. Judging from the chronicler's account, it was more likely to have started as a rowing song. Danish folk poetry has many of these. (See nos. 124, 140, 460, 244, 399) in Grundtvig's *Denmark's Gamle Volkeviser*). The king's boat would be no appropriate place for a festal throng to dramatize a ballad; nor is the refrain "Row, knights, near the land," if it be one, a suitable refrain for a dance song. Cnut's song comes from a date early enough to illustrate ballad origins, but it is of doubtful availability for the communalists. It did not originate in the dance and we do not know that

Here are two songs which are presumably dance songs, from the fifteenth century, the first unusually spirited: [24]

> Icham of Irlaunde,
> Am of the holy londe
> Of Irlande;
> Good sir, pray I ye
> For of Saynte Charite,
> Come ant daunce wyt me
> In Irlaunde.

The second also sounds suitable for its purpose:

> Holi with his mery men they
>   can daunce in hall;
> Ivy & her ientyl women can
>   not daunce at all,
>
> But lyke a meyne of bullokes
>   in a water fall
> Or on a whot somer's day
>   Whan they be mad all.
>
> Nay, nay, ive, it may not be,
>   iwis;
> For holy must haue the mastry,
>   as the maner is.

Neither of these has the stanzaic pattern of the ballads. A song certainly used as a dance song, and very animated and lyrical, is the familiar *The Hunt is Up* of the time of it was, or ever became, a ballad in theme and structure. If it was ever used as a dance song, it was long after it was composed and at the time when — to conform to theories concerning it — it should have been "divorcing itself from the dance" and becoming epic. See *King Cnut's Song and Ballad Origins, Modern Language Notes*, March, 1919.

[24] The first is from MS. Rawlinson, D. 913, f. 1, the second from MS. Balliol, 354, f. 229, b.

Henry VIII. The lines are short, and they throw the hearer into the dancing mood. Some examples of Old' English dance songs, lively and appropriate in melody, coming from the sixteenth century, are given in Chappell's *Old English Popular Music*. An especially popular one was *John, Come Kiss Me Now*.

> Jon come kisse me now, now,
> Jon come kisse me, now,
> Jon, come kisse me by and by,
>   and make no more adow.

The following is a Morris-dance song from Nashe's play of *Summer's Last Will and Testament :* —

> Trip and goe, heave and hoe,
> Up and down, to and fro,
> From the towne to the grove
> Two and two, let us rove,
> A-Maying, a-playing;
> Love hath no gainsaying,
> So merrily trip and goe."

None of these genuine dance songs cited exhibits the septenar rhythm of the ballads; indeed neither the couplet form of the older ballads nor the quartrain form of the newer seems especially appropriate for the dance.

Both nobly-born groups from castle or court and village peasant groups had their dance songs in the Middle Ages; but surely these songs were not contemporaneously of identical type; and it is very improbable that either type was the Child type. There is a great deal of unmistakable testimony as to the use of lyrical, song-like pieces, in England, for dance songs. Next to none exists — not to dwell upon their smaller intrinsic appropriateness — for the staple use of narrative songs for such purpose.

There is evidence, from recent times, that in a few cases well-known Child pieces have been ritualized into dance songs. W. W. Newell speaks of *Barbara Allen* as used in " play party " games in the early part of the nineteenth century in England. This ballad was an actress's song, in the seventeenth century, when we first hear of it. According to Professor Child, *The Maid Freed from the Gallows* has known game-song usage.[25] A version recovered in Nebraska of *The Two Sisters* has obviously been used as a dance song. The following are specimen stanzas :

> There was an old woman lived on the seashore
> > Bow down
> There was an old woman lived on the seashore,
> > Balance true to me
> And she had daughters three or four,
> > Saying I'll be true to my love
> > > If my love is true to me . . .
>
> The oldest and youngest were walking the seashore,
> > Bow down
> The oldest and youngest were walking the seashore,
> > Balance true to me
> The oldest pushed the youngest o'er,
> > Saying I'll be true to my love
> > > If my love is true to me . . .

Such might not have been the case, yet one feels as though, if any of these pieces had been orally preserved for some generations as a dance song, for throngs on the village

[25] See also Gilchrist and Broadwood, *Journal of the Folk-Song Society*, v, pp. 228 ff.

green, the narrative element would have become yet more fragmentary and inconsequential than it is in the quoted dance-song version of *The Two Sisters;* the refrain mean-time assuming greater and greater prominence, and becoming the stable and identifying feature of the song. For dance songs proper, preserved in tradition, one expects a strong refrain formula and a fading or utterly absent narrative element.

That the Child pieces should be utilized, though infrequently, as dance or game songs is not to be wondered at; for popular songs of all kinds are so employed occasionally, alongside the more appropriate inherited dance songs. Mediæval dancing throngs, like their descendants now, were no doubt likely to utilize any new song as a dance song; as *The Hunt is Up,* of the time of Henry VIII, according to *The Complaynt of Scotland* (1549). We are told that in the fast-dying-out play-party or ring-dance songs of our own rural communities, songs like *John Brown's Body, Captain Jinks, Little Brown Jug,* and the negro minstrel *Jim along Jo,* or *Buffalo Gals,* have been so used. Indeed, the minstrel *Old Dan Tucker* has died out of memory as a minstrel song, and has been kept alive as a ring-game song. But if the Child ballads had been dance songs *par excellence,* they would have come down to us very differently in tradition. They played a large rôle in popular recital and song in the Middle Ages, and had the rôle they played as dance songs been proportionately large, we should have unmistakable evidence of it; both external testimonies, and evidence within the songs themselves. We should know from the changes which they developed in structure, from internal allusions to the dance, and from the lore of traditional dance songs.

The dance may well have started many forms of mediæval lyrism with refrain formulas, whether of the artistic or of the more popular type. Such derivation is usually assigned to many of them. But it is the more lyrical forms, rather than the verse-tales, which were most closely bound up with the dance. We also associate with the dance the spontaneous popular lyrics, dance songs proper, which have been preserved for us here and there in printed form, or those which have descended to us in our ring-dance or game songs. Both the art lyrics with refrains, and the more popular and impersonal lyrics with refrains, like *Sumer is icumen in,* make their appearance in literature before ballads of the Child type do.

If dance origin, or connection with the dance, is an essential feature of " ballads," the name belongs with better right to mediæval art lyrics, to the surviving dance songs proper, or to the type remaining in our play-party songs and ring games, for which we have no specific name, aside from the inclusive and ambiguous " folk-song." It is always a safe thing to test our theories as to older conditions for popular song — mediæval conditions, for example — by usages in living society, where these afford analogies; for human procedure, whether in language, action, or song, has remained pretty constant from primitive times onward. The ring games of young people of the present day preserve many of the dramatic elements of the communal dance, and the songs used in them seem to preserve many of the features of the old dance songs. It was the form of these songs, not that of the Child pieces, which was conditioned by dance usage, and bears the marks of such usage. If the Child pieces were primarily evolved in the dance, they ought to show more signs of it, and to be structurally more suitable; for instance, they should suggest more swing and movement. And to think of them as evolved *via* dances of commoners, not of aristocrats, is difficult indeed.

A disciple of the communal theory of ballad origins, Dr. Arthur Saalbach,[26] after special study of the ballad of *Thomas Rymer* (Thomas of Erceldoune) decides that it had its origin in gatherings of the mediaeval dwellers of Earlston for song and dance. They proceeded, he thinks, to give dramatic rendition of the old story of their local hero, Thomas. Some participant improvised a few lines about Thomas to a familiar or an improvised melody. The chorus of bystanders joined in for the refrain or for repetition of the last line of the strophe. Perhaps a man took the rôle of Thomas and a woman the rôle of the Fairy for the whole occasion. The choric-ballad arising in this manner, found favor, and was repeated at the next gathering. He finds additional evidence for such origin in the dramatic handling of the dialogue in the ballad.

But there is nothing suggesting dance-song origin in the structure of *Thomas Rymer,* as it remains to us. It is not even built about a refrain; indeed it seems intrinsically inappropriate as a dance song. And if we argue from the analogies of modern folk-throngs, those at Earlston danced probably to familiar matter — in which case the level of life treated in the subject-matter of their dance song might be higher than their own. Or, if they improvised, their improvisation probably concerned themselves, or something in their immediate horizon, their own

[26] *Entstehungsgeschichte der Schottischen Volksballade, Thomas Rymer.* Diss. Halle (1913), pp. 63–65.

humble interests and station, or the latest occurrence among them. It would not be heroic or a fairy story but something satirical or personal and something contemporary; and, judging from known folk-efforts, it would probably so lack cohesion and finished structure as to be one of the first of their songs to die. *Thomas Rymer* sounds as though composed for the delectation of the aristocratic, not for and certainly not by villagers.

Let us look at some of the dance songs remaining in present tradition, and then apply our observations backward. Children's game songs, and the play-party songs of young folks on the green and in the parlor, in rural communities, have been collected, in England chiefly by Mrs. Gomme, and in the United States by W. W. Newell for New England, and by many collectors for the central west. It is generally agreed that our traditional dance and game songs descend from those of the middle ages and preserve many ancient features; especially the dances in circle form which are executed to the singing of the participants, not to the music of instruments. A number of these pieces seem surely to be of high descent, and many even reflect the old environment of grove and green. Some of the texts sound as though they accompanied the dances of the high born. Recall the many references to " ladies " or " my fair lady "—" lady " is not yet a democratic noun in England — to kings and princes, or dukes, to solid gold rings, to " He wore a star upon his breast," and the like. Most of the songs suggest that they are movement songs by their very wording, or structure. In most cases a typical stanza only will be cited; for the songs are pretty familiar, and they have become accessible,

in late years, in game books for school usage.   The cita-
tions are from Mrs. Gomme's *Dictionary of British Folk-
Lore.*[27]

> Here we go round the mulberry bush,
> The mulberry bush, the mulberry bush,
> Here we go round the mulberry bush,
> On a cold and frosty morning.
>
> > *Mulberry Bush,* I, p. 404.

> Round and round the village,
> Round and round the village,
> Round and round the village,
> As we have done before.

> In and out the windows,
> In and out the windows,
> In and out the windows,
> As we have done before.
>
> > *Round and Round the Village,* II, p. 122.

> Tripping up the green grass,
>   Dusty, dusty day,
> Come all ye pretty fair maids,
>   Come and with me play. . . .

> Naughty man, he won't come out,
>   He won't come out, he won't come out,

[27] Mrs. Gomme gives a list of dance games, II, p. 465, and of
circle-form games, with singing and action, II, p. 476.   The songs
cited here are recognized by her as descending in traditional dance
usage.

"In den Kinderreigen," says Böhme, *Geschichte des Tanzes,* ch.
XVII, "werden wir noch alten Überresten von Tanzliedern der Vor-
zeit begegnen."   As ring-dances were given up by the mature they
lingered among children.   One should not infer, however, that *all*
children's play songs were originally game or dance-songs of grown-
ups.   Childhood is as ancient as maturity, and even the savagest
children have their own songs.

Naughty man, he won't come out,
  To help us in our dancing.
                        Green Grass, i, p. 156.

From another text of the same song:

Here we go up the green grass,
The green grass, the green grass,
Here we go up the green grass,
So early in the morning.

                        Ibid., i, p. 160.

A ring, a ring o' roses,
A pocket full of posies;
A curtsey in and a curtsey out,
And a curtsey all together.

                        A Ring of Roses, ii, p. 108.

Green gravel green gravel, the grass is so green,
The fairest young damsel that ever was seen. . . .
                        Green Gravel, i, p. 171.

The material is too abundant and too familiar for much
illustration to be needed. A few more miscellaneous
stanzas are:

Here we come a-piping,
First in spring and then in May,
The Queen she sits upon the sand,
Fair as a lily, white as a wand:
King John has sent you letters three,
And begs you'll read them unto me,
We can't read one without them all,
So, pray, Miss Bridget, deliver the ball.

                        Queen Anne, ii, p. 91.

Here's a soldier left his lone,
Wants a wife and can't get none,
Merrily go round and choose your own,

Choose a good one or else choose none,
Choose the worst or choose the best,
Or choose the very one you like best.

> *Here's a Soldier*, I, p. 206.

Poor Mary, what're you weepin' for,
A-weepin' for, a-weepin' for,
Pray, Mary, what're you weepin' for?
On a bright summer's day.

> *Poor Mary Sits A-Weeping*, II, p. 47.

The following dramatic song is listed by Mrs. Gomme as a circle-form song; though she thinks it originally a harvest-song:

Oats and beans and barley grow!
Oats and beans and barley grow!
Do you or I or anyone know
How oats and beans and barley grow?
First the farmer *sows* his seed,
Then he *stands* and takes his ease,
Stamps his foot, and *claps* his hands,
Then *turns round* to view the land
Waiting for a partner, waiting for a partner!
Open the ring and take one in.

> *Oats and Beans and Barley*, II, p. 1.

Let us turn next to some of the ring-dance songs of young people in the United States, surviving in our fast-dying-out play-party songs. The dancing, as in the mediæval dance songs, is to the singing of the dancers, not to instrumental music. Old World importations are easily recognized. The refrains remain the same as in their British cognates:

Come honey, my love, come trip with me,
In the morning early

Heart and hand we'll take our stand;
'Tis true, I love you dearly.

Weevilly Wheat.[28]

Oh, the jolly old miller boy, he lived by the mill,
The mill turned round with a right good will,
 And all that he made, he put it on the shelf,
At the end of the year he was gaining in his wealth,
One hand in the hopper, and the other in the sack,
Gents step forward and the ladies step back.

The Jolly Old Miller.[29]

Go out and in the window,
Go out and in the window,
Go out and in the window,
 For we shall gain the day.

We're Marching Round the Levy.[30]

Lost your partner, what'll you do?
Lost your partner, what'll you do?
Lost your partner, what'll you do?
Skip to My Lou, my darling.

Skip to My Lou.[31]

Come all ye young people that's wending your way,
And sow your wild oats in your youthful day,
For the daylight it passes, and night's coming on,
So choose you a partner, and be marching along, marching
 along.[32]

Professor E. F. Piper points out [33] that in songs which

[28] Mrs. L. D. Ames, *The Missouri Play-Party, Journal of American Folk-Lore,* XXIV (1911), p. 302.

[29] *Ibid.,* p. 306.

[30] *Ibid.,* p. 306.

[31] *Ibid.,* p. 304.

[32] *Ibid.,* p. 314.

[33] *Some Play-Party Games of the Middle West, Journal of American Folk-Lore,* CIX, p. 264.

describe the progress of a game, like *The Miller Boy* (*The Jolly Miller* of Mrs. Gomme) and *Juniper Tree:*

> O dear sister Phoebe, how happy were we,
> The night we sat under the juniper tree!
> The juniper tree, heigho, heigho!
> The juniper tree, heigho!
>
> Then rise you up, Sister, go choose you a man,
> Go choose you the fairest that ever you can,
> Then rise you up, Sister, and go, and go,
> Then rise you up, Sister, and go. . . .

the form remains fairly constant. In such songs one cannot easily change the words without changing the formula. In the same way, *Oats, pease, beans,* remains fairly constant. *Weevilly Wheat* and *Kilmacrankie* perhaps afford examples of " the decay of ballad matter under the usage of the singing game, or dance."[34] Many of the songs he lists show the influence of quadrilles and other dances, illustrating once more the tendency of the imported, or higher, or newer, to descend and linger among the humbler and more remote. A few more illustrations of genuine communal dance songs should suffice:

> We come here to bounce around,
> We come here to bounce around,
> We come here to bounce around,
>   Tra, la, la, la!
>   Ladies, do, si, do,
>   Gents, you know,

[34] This seems the natural process; but compare Professor Gummere's latest theories of ballad growth and "improvement," cited a little farther on. The process which, to collectors of folk dance-songs, brings ballad degradation, to Professor Gummere is the process by which are evolved "good" ballads. At other times, however,

Swing to the right,
And then to the left,
And all promenade.[35]

Up and down the center we go,
Up and down the center we go,
Up and down the center we go,
This cold and frosty morning.

Chase that Squirrel.[36]

When popular songs, or street songs, are utilized as
dance songs, they are handled like this:

Captain Jinks

I'm Captain Jinks of the horse marines,
I feed my horse on corn and beans,
And court young ladies in their teens,
For that's the style of the army.

We'll all go round and circle left,
We'll circle left, we'll circle left,
We'll all go round and circle left,
For that's the style of the army.
The ladies right and form a ring,
And when they form you give'm a swing,
And when you swing you give'm a call,
And take your lady and promenade all.[37]

Jim Along Jo

Hi, Jim along, Jim along, Josie
Hi, Jim along, Jim, along Jo
Hi, Jim along, Jim along Josie
Hi, Jim along, Jim along Jo.[38]

he continued to make reference to the " degradation " and " decay "
due to tradition.

[35] Ames, p. 296.

[36] Piper, p. 266.

[37] Ames, p. 309.

[38] Piper, p. 268.

Little Brown Jug

Sent my brown jug down in town,
Sent my brown jug down in town,
Sent my brown jug down in town,
So early in the morning.[39]

Not one of these pieces is a ballad, just as the vocal accompaniments to old British dances round the Maypole were not ballads. One of the latter has survived in the ring games of the Georgia negroes, again illustrating the survival, in outlying places, among the humble and remote, of matter assimilated from the usage, in bygone vogue, of people of another social class:

All around the May-pole,
    The May-pole, the May-pole,
All around the May-pole.
    Now, Miss Sally, won't you bow? etc.[40]

Repetition and interweaving of lines, is much more pervasive and essential in communal dance songs than in pieces of the Child type, and it is of a different kind. It shows us, however, the type of repetition to be expected in such dance songs. There is no evidence that ballads are ever built up from dance songs, but a great deal that dance songs may be built upon popular songs of all types. Mrs. Gomme notes that many English circle-game songs have evidently been derived from love ballads, drinking songs, and toasts, and that some of the dance games are of this origin.

[39] Goldy M. Hamilton, *The Play-Party in Northeast Missouri*, *Journal of American Folk-Lore*, xxvii, pp. 269, 297 (*The Girl I Left Behind Me*), p. 301.

[40] Loraine Darby, *Ring Games from Georgia*, *Journal of American Folk-Lore*, xxx (1917), p. 218.

If the ballads had been used typically in popular dances, collections like those made by Mrs. Gomme and Mr. Newell should reveal many traces of such usage. On the other hand, when we do not assume that ballads were the staple material of mediæval dance songs, what has come down to us in tradition is of just the character which we should expect. There are many " situation " songs among these traditional dance and game songs, and there are dialogue pieces; [41] but one finds no traces of the development of dialogue songs into ballads proper, or of the " divorcing " of dance songs from the dance, on the way toward becoming lyric-epics.

When we examine genuine dance songs, it becomes clear that their most important element is the repetitional element. The texts of most of them shift even more than do the ballad texts, for there is no story to hold them together; but the repeated element, or the refrain, is stable.[42] They are lyrical, and they tempt to movement. And, as suggested above, no matter how long they have been preserved in usage as dance songs, they have never developed into anything like Child ballads, nor have they been transformed into narrative pieces of any type. They show no signs of the evolution sketched by Professor Gum-

[41] Mrs. Gomme thinks that the dialogue songs are of later development, II, p. 500. Professors W. M. Hart and G. H. Stempel think that dialogue songs represent a very early stage, in the history of ballads proper.

[42] A remark made by Professor C. S. Baldwin concerning the ballad is much truer of the dance song, " The refrain, then, is not a poetic embellishment; it is a kind of nucleus; it determines the structure. The tale is built around the refrain," *English Mediæval Literature* (1914), p. 237. For the rôle played by refrains in the English ballads, see p. 188.

mere, in his chapter in the *Cambridge History of English Literature:*

The structure of the ballad — what makes it a species, the elements of it — derives from choral and dramatic conditions; what gives it its peculiar art of narrative is the epic process working by oral tradition and gradually leading to a new structure.

Or in his *The Popular Ballad:* [43]

. . . the course of the popular ballad is from a mimetic choral situation, slowly detaching itself out of the festal dance and coming into the reminiscent ways of tradition in song and recital.

Or in *Democracy and Poetry:*

Development of narrative poetry out of repetition is an obvious process easily proved by the facts and consists simply in a decrease of verbal repetition and a corresponding increase of the verbal increment." . . . " An epic element, accretional and explanatory, has in many cases been added to the choral and dramatic nucleus." [44]

The songs cited in the foregoing pages have survived under the right conditions, oral and communal, but they show no signs of an " epic process " leading to a new structure. The Child ballads, on the other hand, show something quite different from the dance songs. For them, the refrain is the variable element. Their texts

[43] P. 84. It is rather surprising to find, on pp. 68–69, that "narrative is not a fixed fundamental primary fact in the ballad scheme." This means that the very thing that makes a ballad a ballad, not verse of some other lyric type, is not a fundamental or primary feature of its structure.

[44] Pp. 186, 190.

remain as constant as the conditions of transmission allow; but the refrain does not remain constant within the same ballad. The test of living folk-song, examination of the kind of thing which the folk can improvise now, and the character of the songs which are genuinely and primarily dance songs, preserved in oral transmission, ought to show the fatuity of seeking an identical genesis for these types and for pieces like the English and Scottish popular ballads.[45] It is a safer hypothesis that the Child type of piece, once established in popularity, might at times be fitted to well-known dance tunes, or be utilized, like nearly any other kind of song, as a dance song, than that dance-genesis evolved the Child type — that the Child type represents, *par excellence* among poetic types, an evolution from dance origin.

III — NARRATIVE SONGS AND THE DANCE

It would be going much too far, would indeed be contrary to the facts, to affirm that there is never dancing to narrative songs. Among European peoples where the narrative song has established itself as a leading type of popular song, instances of it occur, and there should be occasional instances of it anywhere among advanced peoples.[46] This should be especially true of the shorter

[45] Andrew Lang, in his article on Ballads in the *Encyclopædia Britannica* wrote: "It is natural to conclude that our ballads too were first improvised and circulated in rustic dances." He held at the time the views still held by the majority of American scholars. But in his article on the same subject in the last edition of Chambers's *Cyclopædia of English Literature* (1904), he has given up this theory of ballad origins, and indeed, from his article, is hardly recognizable as still a communalist.

[46] "Narrative, too, are most of the dance songs in a modern

and more tuneful ballads. There was perhaps some dancing to heroic narrative songs, if not to "histories," probably to romantic tales, in England. We have seen that in American ring-dance or "play-party" games, the descendants of mediæval dance-modes, narrative songs are utilized occasionally, as *Barbara Allen's Cruelty,* referred to earlier, to accompany the dance. Songs of all types have undergone this experience, probably ballads along with the others, especially when the words were fitted to some familiar dance tune. But in a majority of cases the narrative pieces would be less suitable. Such utilization — this is my point — would not represent an original stage, but would be exceptional rather than normal.

Our best evidence for early European dance songs comes from France. The French dance songs which remain to us are lyric, not lyric-epic, and they are aristocratic.[47] Indeed, admits Professor Gummere, " all the Old French

Russian cottage," writes Professor Gummere, *Old English Ballads,* p. lxxix, and cites Ralston, *Songs of the Russian People,* 1872. But the examples given by Ralston are not narrative; they are not ballads but lyrics, and of the expected type. Professor Gummere's solitary example of a dance ballad is from the Ditmarsh folk of Holstein, but even that is more lyric than lyric-epic. It labels itself as a dance song, and might well be an older song which has been fitted to the dance, not one made in the dance. *The Popular Ballad,* p. 97, footnote.

Strictly, what are called " dances " among savages are in large part drama, and there is abundance of histrionic or mimetic action accompanied by songs of which action is the illustration, *i. e.,* there are songs suggesting ideas, and these are to some extent enacted. Over against these are the rhythmic chants and ejaculatory refrains that form simple motor suggestions or reverberations. The latter are the only ones " danced " in our modern sense of " dance."

[47] Jeanroy, *Les Origines de la Poésie Lyrique en France au Moyen Age,* 1904; Bédier, *Les Plus Anciennes Danses Françaises, Revue des Deux Mondes,* Jan. 15, 1906, p. 398.

dances were aristocratic to the point of making modern
investigators doubt the existence of the ' popular ' cus-
toms." [48]   English dance songs have already been exam-
ined.   Let us turn to Icelandic usage.   Vigfusson [49] tells
us that the " dance, in full use accompanied by songs
which are described as loose and amorous " — lyrical
pieces these seem to be — appears at the end of the eleventh
century.   Icelandic *danz* comes to mean song; and *flimt,*
loose song, and *danz* are synonymous words.   The *rimur,*
or epical paraphrases, with matter like that of our ballads,
first appear about the middle of the fourteenth century.
Almost all Icelandic sagas and romances, even the histor-
ical books of the Bible, were turned, we are told, into such
lays or ballads.   " The heathen heroic poems were cer-
tainly never used," says Vigfusson, " to accompany a
dance.   Their flow and meter are a sufficient proof of
that."   The word *dance* points, wherever found, to a new
fashion introduced from France and spreading quickly
over Europe.   The old words would not serve for this
new French art, which brought its own name even to Ice-
land.   Icelandic evidence is the earliest that we have for
the dance songs of Scandinavian countries, and the early
Icelandic dance songs were, it would appear, lyrical and
amatory, like the early French and English dance songs.
The employment of heroic romantic narrative material
belongs to a later stage.

In Denmark, courtly society of the later middle ages
danced to narrative ballads, and the pieces closely resemble
the Child ballads.   But Danish literature seems to know
no other song, no body of purely lyrical movement songs.

[48] *The Popular Ballad,* p. 97.
[49] Cleasby-Vigfusson, *Icelandic Dictionary,* under *danz.*

The wealth of lyric poetry appearing in England and France and Germany was unknown in Denmark. It has no erotic lyric poetry. The ballad was practically the only form, we are told, in which the people expressed their feelings. The Danish ballads are very valuable. " We possess," says Steenstrup, " 40 ballad manuscripts of the period prior to 1750, while Sweden possesses 10, the oldest antedated by many Danish." The Danish ballads were preserved by high-born ladies of the sixteenth and seventeenth centuries, who did fine service in collecting into manuscripts the songs current in the castles of the period.

The Danish pieces show their connection with the dance, as do most dance songs, in their very texts, and they even show how the dance was conducted. Here are some specimen lines: [50]

> Midsummer night upon the sward,
> Knights and squires were standing guard.
>
> In the grove a knightly dance they tread
> With torches and garlands of roses red.
>
> In sable and martin before them all
> Dances Sir Iver, the noblest of all.
>
> To the king in his tower strong
> Floats the noise of the dancing throng.
>
> " Who is yon knight that leads the dance,
> And louder than all the song he chants?"
>
> *Proud Elselille,* No. 220.

[50] These and other examples are cited by Steenstrup, *The Mediæval Popular Ballad,* p. 12. Translated by E. G. Cox.

> Now longs the king himself
>   To step the dance;
> The hero Hagen follows after,
>   For them the song he chants.
> *So stately dances Hagen.*
>
> *Hagen's Dance*, No. 465.

> It was Mettelil, the count's daughter,
> She stepped the dance for them.
>
> No. 261.

> There dances Sir Stig, as light as a wand,
> With a silver cup in his white hand.
>
> No. 76.

Individual ballads reveal by internal testimony that they were used for the dance:

> Step lightly o'er the green plain —
> The maid must follow me;
>
> No. 241.

> Step up boldly, young knight;
> Honor the maidens in the dance.
>
> No. 244.

> Stand up, stand up, my maidens all,
> And dance for me a space;
> And sing for me a ballad
> About the sons of Lave's race.
>
> No. 366.

An account of the Ditmarsh folk of Holstein by Johann Adolfi (Neocorus) written in 1598, says that the people have *adapted nearly all their songs to the dance, in order to remember them better, and to keep them current.*[51]

[51] *Chronik des Landes Dithmarschen*, edited by F. C. Dahlmann, I, p. 177; "Nichtess weiniger isst tho vorwunderen (den up dat de

The dances he describes are like the Danish dances, with singing by a " foresinger," and choral response and refrain. There were also, as in our own ring-dance songs, whole pieces where all the participants sang as they danced.

There is little or nothing of the Danish type of self-labeled dance songs among the Child pieces. All but a few of the Danish ballads have refrains. Those lacking them are mostly late importations or translations. The movement is often nimble and rapid. On the other hand, of 1250 versions of the English ballads, about 300, i. e., a fourth, have refrains.[52]

As to origins, the Danish ballads do not help the communalists, but the contrary. The dancing for which they were used — some were employed for entertainment of other kinds, like riding or rowing — was the dancing of the high-born; both in content and movement, they seem suitable for this purpose. Both Grundtvig and Steenstrup seem to be satisfied with the hypothesis of minstrel authorship for them. They offer no suggestion of the responsibility, for the type, of festal village throngs, or of the throngs of primitive times. And it is interesting to note that when Steenstrup seeks to restore the Danish ballads to their older and truer form, and to rid them of spurious accretions, one of his first steps is to shear away various types of repetition, as " padding." [53]

Gesenge edder Geschichte deste ehr gelehret unnd beter beholden worden unnd lenger im Gebruke bleven, hebben se de alle fast den Dentzen bequemet), dat se nha Erfordering der Wortt und Wise des Gesanges," etc.

[52] The Popular Ballad, p. 74.

[53] The Mediæval Popular Ballad, pp. 75–77.

At this point, something should, no doubt, be said with reference to the ballads of the Faroe Islands. They have been brought much into the foreground, in the discussions of the genesis of the ballads, and afford to communalists their chief stronghold; [54] although Steenstrup advises caution [55] in using them for help in understanding older ballad forms. Their recollection of Saga and Eddic poetry is strong, and this knowledge must have blended with knowledge of the poetry of the middle ages. Moreover popular ballads, he says, were taken up by priests and learned people. Several types of verse are to be noted in Faroe folk-song; but mostly the introduction of Danish ballads, supposed to have begun in the sixteenth century, has affected them. In the Faroes, in the preceding century at least, as, in less degree, in our own fast-dying-out ring-game or play-party songs of young people, throng dancing of the old circle type, with linked hands, was still preserved. The dancing is to singing rather than to instrumental music, again as in our ring-games; and as in the latter, all take part in the singing and all join in the refrain. Sometimes spontaneous improvised lines or verses, still as in our ring-games, arise out of the occasion itself.

The classic report of the Faroe dances was made by Pastor Lyngbye in 1822, who left descriptions of them. Their dance-themes are derived from Norwegian or Icelandic sources, a favorite subject being the "hero

---

[54] "The ballad-genesis is more plainly proved for the Faroes than for any other modern people" (Gummere, *The Popular Ballad*, p. 69).

[55] See *The Mediæval Popular Ballad*, p. 7.

Sigurd." They dance to historical ballads, like the Danes,[56] but to religious and lampooning ballads as well. There are many lyric-epics, like the Danish ones we have mentioned. Indeed, the Icelanders know and use ballads in the Danish language. The fishermen also have rude dances, sometimes to songs of their own creation. Pastor Lyngbye tells of one, often utilized for argument by Professor Gummere, concerning a fisherman, pushed by his comrades into the center of the throng, while they improvised verses upon a recent mishap which had befallen him. The text of the song is not preserved, so we cannot place its type. We have no right to call it a ballad; most probably it was not. From what we are told of them, these improvised fishermen pieces sound analogous to our own ranch-hand, cowboy, lumberman, or negro improvisations, or to the occasional spontaneous ventures of our own ring-dances. They are upon events of the moment, of interest to members of the circle involved. They are fashioned on or are imitations of, songs of better type, of higher descent, and they are markedly crude and poor. Further, the Faroe fishermen pieces are sung to hymn tunes or to familiar airs, not to invented melodies, or to traditional melodies — not at least to melodies traditional

[56] Our earliest testimony concerning the Faroe dances is to be found in the *Faroa Reserata* of Lucas Debes, Kopenhagen, 1673. He writes, p. 251, that "the inhabitants of the Faroe Islands are little inclined toward useless pastimes or idle gaiety, but content themselves mostly with singing psalms . . . only at marriages or at Christmas time do they seek amusement in a simple circle dance, one grasping another by the hand while they sing old hero-songs." Pastor Lyngbye's much-quoted *Færøiske Quæder*, etc., was published in 1822. See also N. Annandale, *The Faroes and Iceland*, Oxford, 1905. The whole matter of Faroe folk-song was cleared up satisfactorily by H. Thuren in his *Folke Saangen paa Færøerne*, 1908.

from ancient times.[57]   The Faroe songs teach us nothing
as to the genesis of the lyric-epic type, for they them-
selves preserve and continue imported fashions.   All in
all, there is nothing to be learned from the Faroe dance-
song customs that runs contrary to evidence from other
sources.   Rather do they bear it out.   And certainly we
cannot look to them as mirroring *par excellence* what is
oldest.[58]

[57] The type of song now used by Shakers, Holy Rollers, and other
dancing religious sects ought to be a point of corroborative interest.
They probably resemble the Salvation Army type of hymn.

[58] For German, an excellent display of dance-song material may be
found in Franz Böhme's *Geschichte des Tanzes in Deutschland*,
Leipzig, 1886.   In chapter xv, "über Tanzlieder," he groups his
material into classes, to show the varied character of the content.
He gives amatory songs first place, as the most frequent accompani-
ment of the dance, with many examples.   Historical songs, old hero
songs, and mythic pieces (his second class), were sung, he thinks,
in the oldest period, for the dance.   But his evidence for this is the
hero songs of the Faroes, concerning which we have evidence from
the seventeenth century, and the testimony of Neocorus (1598) con-
cerning the Ditmarsh folk of Holstein.   The bearing of this evidence
has already been considered.   The third class he names consists of
ballads or epic folk-songs, for which his examples for Germany are
meager.   This class, he says, was "in full bloom" in the Romance
languages and in England, as sung at the dance — a hasty and mis-
taken generalization.   A fourth class consists of lampoons, vitupera-
tions, satires, etc., abundantly illustrated.   This is the class of dance
songs which is often improvised.   His next class consists of bird
and animal songs, as of the nightingale, cuckoo, heron, owl, fox, etc.
Riddle, wishing, and wager songs, and (rarely) religious songs con-
stitute the last classes.   In the second part of his history, the author
prints 356 specimens of dance songs and melodies, in chronological
sequence.   Among these illustrative dance songs the epic folk-song,
the ballad of the Child type, is the type playing the least conspicuous
rôle.   How any scholar who examines Böhme's display of mediæval
dance-song material — it is strikingly parallel to English dance-song
material — can retain the belief that lyric-epic pieces like the Child

In the Child pieces, the story, not suggestion of move-
ment or suitability for movement, is the main thing.
When a refrain is present, the only sure inference to be
made from its presence is that the piece was made to be
sung, or possibly to be recited orally.   The refrain is
present in mediæval as in modern songs which have no
connection with the dance.   But the refrain itself is not
an essential in the Child pieces as it is in the Danish;
we have just pointed out that hardly a fourth, by Profes-
sor Gummere's count, have refrains.   In those which are
surely old, like *The Battle of Otterbourne, The Hunting
of the Cheviot,* or *Judas,* no refrain is present.   It is not
then a constant feature, but occurs variably.   Nor is it
constant even for individual ballads, but fluctuates, appar-
ently, with the melodies to which they were sung.   If the
Child ballad, or its archetype, was a dance song, the refrain
formula ought to persist above all else, through oral tradi-

pieces were conditioned first of all by mediæval dances, is hard to
understand.   They seem to be a lyric type least to be associated with
such usage.

It is true that Professor Böhme, whose book was published in
1886, begins with the view that "Tanzlieder waren die ersten
Lieder," "Beim Tanze wurden die ältesten epischen Dichtungen
(erzählende Volkslieder) gesungen, durch den Tanz sind sie veran-
lasst worden . . .," "Die älteste Poesie eines jeden Volkes ist eine
Verbindung von Tanz, Spiel, und Gesang."   But his material does
not bear out his preliminary statements, nor is he insistent upon the
narrative song as the earliest dance song, as his book proceeds.
He tells us, p. 230, that we learn the origin and the form of dance
songs best from the South German *Schnadahüpfln,* short two- or
four-line songs, to familiar melodies, often improvised (see his
fourth class) by singers and dancers.   Among these songs, the he-
roic element hardly appears, and the historic never.   A careful
survey of the citations in Böhme's *Geschichte des Tanzes* should
disillusion believers in the ballad as the characteristic type of medi-
æval dance song, or as the leading lyric type of dance genesis.

tion and dance usage, as it does in the dance or ring-game songs of which we are sure. It is what should identify the individual ballads. Moreover, refrains appear very abundantly in the later pieces and in broadsides; that is, they are not distanced, the farther we get from the hypothetical dance-throngs with which they are supposed to be bound up.

When the English and Scottish ballads do use the refrain, they use it in the art way, not in the folk way. It is something extraneous, introduced from the outside, varying for the same ballad, subject to modification or replacement at the will of the singers, not part of the fabric of the song. And like the refrains of the art songs of the middle ages, carols, or roundels, or *ballades,* it comes at regular intervals. It is not handled like the repetitions of traditional dance songs, usually the most stable element of the song, nor in the crude way of much of the repetition in unlettered folk-improvisations. Nor should it be confused with the one-word and two-word songs chanted in the choral repetitions of savage tribes. The latter are not refrains, but the whole song.

Refrains and choral repetitions are more necessary to other kinds of mediæval lyric verse than they are to ballads. It is not, in fact, the presence of a refrain, or of choral repetition that makes the Child pieces ballads. What is essential, if pieces are to be classified as ballads, is that they tell a story in verse. If they are ballads of the Child type they probably exhibit structural or lyrical repetition in their presentation of narrative material; but no amount of structural or lyrical repetition makes a piece a ballad unless a narrative element is present. Repetition of both types is a striking characteristic, for example, of

revival hymns, and these had their origin neither as
ballads nor as dance songs,[59] and it is characteristic, most
of all, of game and dance songs proper; yet these are not
ballads. In practice, it is conceded by everybody, com-
munalists too, that a lyric may have a refrain, or repeated
lines, as do many of the lyrics from the Elizabethan
dramatists, yet not be a ballad. *Sumer is icumen in* has
a refrain, but is not a ballad; the Bannockburn song has
a refrain, but is not a ballad. On the other hand, a lyric
may have no refrain or choral repetition, like *King Est-
mere,* or *Thomas Rymer,* yet be a ballad. As already
pointed out, the name ballad attached itself to a type
of lyric which is pretty far removed from the mediæval
lyric type of early dance employment. If we are to insist
on a dance element in a lyric which we are to classify
as a ballad, we might apply the name, with better right,
to art lyrics, or to folk lyrics of the fluid traditional
type, held to unity and memorableness by the refrain,
which persist in the ring-games of young people and in
children's songs; or we should restrict it to genuine dance
songs, of which we have many of equal age with the
majority of ballads which have come down to us.

In the English and Scottish ballads, dancing plays
hardly any rôle. It is referred to a fair number of times;
but as a recreation for the lords and ladies who appear
in the ballads it plays a less striking part than does the
game of ball, its rival and a recreation with which it was

[59] Compare " Incremental repetition made up the whole frame
of *The Maid Freed from the Gallows* simply because such ballads
were still part and parcel of the dance " (*The Popular Ballad,* p.
117). Repetition is emphasized as the most characteristic feature of
ballads, pp. 117–134, etc.

often combined. It is far less frequent than reference
to songs and to minstrelsy. Mostly the allusions are to
dancing of the more modern type, accompanied by the
music of instruments; and they bear testimony to the
coming of dance-modes from France. A few typical pas-
sages are the following:

> Seek no minstrels to play, mother,
>   No dancers to dance in your room;
> But tho your son comes, Leesome Brand,
>   Yet he comes sorry to the town.
>
> *Leesome Brand.*

> There was two little boys going to the school,
>   And twa little boys they be,
> They met three brothers playing at the ba,
>   And ladies dancing, hey.
>
> *The Two Brothers.*

> I'm gauin, I'm gauin,
>   I'm gauin to Fraunce, lady,
> When I come back,
>   I'll learn ye a dance, lady.
>
> *Rob Roy.*

Another text ends:

> I hae been in foreign lands,
>   And served the King o' France, ladie;
> We will get bagpipes,
>   And we'll hae a dance, ladie.

Or:

> Get dancers here to dance, she sais,
>   And minstrels for to play;
> For here's my young son, Florentine,
>   Come here wi me to stay.
>
> *The Earl of Mar's Daughter.*

Two might have reference to dancing of the older type:

> Her father led her through the ha'
> Her mither danced before them a'.
>
> *The Cruel Brother.*

> When dinner it was past and done,
>   And dancing to begin
> We'll go take the bride's maidens,
>   And we'll go fill the ring.

> O ben then cam the auld French lord,
>   Saying, Bride, will ye dance with me?
> " Awa, awa, ye auld French lord,
>   Your face I wowna see."
>
> *Fair Janet.*

Fair Janet, with its theme of probation by dancing, closely resembles certain Scandinavian and German ballads, but has lessened the part played by the dance test.

The internal evidence that the English and Scottish ballads were used as dance songs is very meager, compared, for example, with the very abundant internal evidence that they were sung. But in practice, few scholars would now make special claim that they were used as dance songs. No doubt they were, here and there, as in late times, we have seen, were *Barbara Allen* and *The Two Sisters,* in this country. The refrains of several might connect them with the dance, as Mrs. Brown's *The Bonny Birdy* (no. 82), or *The Maid and the Palmer* (no. 21). But most sound more suitable for recital or singing than to accompany rhythmic motion. Fitted to dance tunes they might be used as dance songs, but typically they were composed for other purposes. It is pretty hard for the student of real dance song to feel that the mass of the Child pieces, or their archetypes, developed from the folk-dance. Mediæval rural throngs, like their descendants to-day, probably danced mostly to something already familiar, and in itself suitable; more rarely they may have danced to their own spontaneous but inconsequential and impermanent improvisations. The typical mediæval dance song was, however, more lyric than epic. The English and Scottish ballads are as epic as they are lyric.

There is a classic passage in *The Complaynt of Scotland,*[60] 1549, by which we can check pretty well our assumptions and conclusions. The author of *The Complaynt* makes his " shepherds " (pretty literary and classical shepherds they are, genuine shepherds of the " Golden Age ") tell tales, sing songs, and afterwards dance in a ring. Among the 48 *tales* with which they amused themselves, alongside Chaucer's *Canterbury Tales,* Arthurian romance, and classical stories, as of Hercules, or of Hero and Leander, are listed the tale of " robene hude and litil ihone," and the tale of the " zong tamlene " (Tamlane). Among the 36 *songs,* are the Henry VIII *Pastance with gude companye, The frog cam to the myl dur, The battel of the hayrlau,* and *The hunttis of cheuet* — probably the song that Sidney praised; also *The perssee and the mongumrye met,* i. e., *The Battle of Otterbourne.* The Child pieces referred to thus far have been either told or sung, as we should expect. Then comes a list of 30 *dance* pieces — most of them obviously such, as *Al cristyn mennis dance, The gosseps dance, The alman haye, The dance of kyrlrynne, Schaik a trot,* etc. The

⁶⁰ Edited by J. A. H. Murray, for the Early English Text Society, 1872, vol. 1, p. 63.

list is headed by *The Hunt Is Up,* the tune of which is
well fitted for dancing. No Child pieces appear. Num-
ber 92, *Robene hude,* is probably a *chanson de Robin* (see
Cotgrave), or Robin Hood and Maid Marian piece.
There were many Robin Hood dances, and they are not to
be identified with the Robin Hood ballads. Number 93,
Thom of lyn, is not the ballad *Tamlane,* listed among the
recited pieces, but the very different and wholly appro-
priate song of *Young Thomlin,* licensed in 1557–58.
Number 108, *Ihonne ermistrangis dance,* is the one pos-
sible Child piece of the 30; but neither Mr. Furnivall nor
Mr. Murray believes it to be identical with any of the
four ballads involving Armstrongs (*Johnny Armstrong,
Johnny Armstrong's Last Goodnight, Jock o' the Side,
Dick of the Cow*) which have come down to us. The
Armstrong ballads in Child's collection are hardly suitable
as dance songs.

Should not the *Complaynt's* roll of tales, songs, and
dance songs, read very differently, had the English and
Scottish ballads been the typical songs for the dances of
rural throngs? The ballads which are mentioned are not
mentioned as dance songs, and they are in highly literary
and aristocratic company. The dance songs which are
mentioned seem to be exactly of the suitable type which
we should expect.

Much dance-song material, primitive, mediæval, and
modern — the latter in our still-existent ring-dance songs
— is available, from which to make observation and to
generalize. The tendencies to be inferred from it are
exactly the reverse of those assumed by Professor Gum-
mere, and currently accepted in America.[61]

[61] That belief in dance origin, emergence from the illiterate, com-

1. When songs already existent are used as communal dance songs, they tend to retrograde to simple repetitions of striking lines or titles. If narrative, they are likely to lose the story. As for primitive dance songs, they are never narrative.

2. The repetitions of communal dance songs are much more abundant than the repetitions of the ballads, and they belong more genuinely to the fabric of the song. They are not of the symmetrical art type, of regular recurrence, the refrain type proper, but are cruder, or more pervading. Often some striking formula recurs over and over, and is the main song. For ballads proper, the refrain is not the most stable element but the most fluctuating.

3. There is no tendency for dance songs, whether situation songs or dialogue songs, to develop epic elements or to become " refined and ennobled by tradition," *i. e.*, to become real ballads.[62] Real ballads used as dance songs tend to decay, through the wearing process of dance usage. Songs used as dance songs do not tend to develop into ballads, but rather to become simplified to some striking line or formula.

4. As regards form, genuine communal dance songs are not necessarily or invariably in ballad stanza, but of

munal improvisation, epic development, and the priority of dialogue and situation songs, has current American acceptance, is shown by the fact that such belief is set forth, without hesitation or question, in the two latest American ballad anthologies: Professor W. M. Hart's *English Popular Ballads*, 1916, and Professor G. H. Stempel's *A Book of Ballads*, 1917.

[62] Gummere, *The Popular Ballad*, p. 76, " The refining and ennobling processes of tradition " . . . " ennobled and enriched in its traditional course," p. 28, etc.

more fluid and variable pattern. They exhibit no one fixed stanzaic type. Sometimes they consist of but one short stanza.

We are hardly justified by the evidence, then, in saying that the English ballads represent a lyric type which has been " divorced from the dance, originally their vital condition." The process is not that ballads, originating in the dance, find permanence and gain epic character when cut loose from it. Rather do already existing ballads find themselves utilized for, adapted to, and mutilated in dance song usage. There is no testimony that the structure of the English ballads rests upon the dance, but rather the contrary; for theirs is not the structure of the normal and more appropriate dance song. That the dance songs of primitive peoples, and the earliest dance songs that we have in English, and our latest surviving dance songs are all three lyric, not lyric-epic, does not point to the origin of the English ballad type by " divorce from the dance."

There are three forms of psychic suggestion in poetry; first, emotional, as in the simple lyric; second, ideational, as in the narrative; third, motor, as in the refrain type, coupled with simple imperatives. The first and second types may be associated with action in the sense of conduct, and they are so associated in primitive poetry. They are sometimes continued traditionally in what are called " dances," but are really drama; that is, they become histrionic. The third type is the only form fundamentally associated with the dance, and it is psychologically simple, i. e., *presentative* not *representative*. This psychical distinction should be borne in mind in study of the subject. Not all lyrics tempt to movement, and narratives (ballads proper) never, one would think, tempt to *measured move-ment* of the dance type.

Association with the dance of the festal multitude may be in place for the French *ballade,* or for the Italian *ballata,* but our own ballads do not include pieces which were primarily dance songs. That the English ballad type had its genesis in the folk-dance seems to be not only unproved but unlikely. Those who believe in dance gen-esis for the lyric in general may find in the dance the ultimate genesis of the lyric-epic type which we call ballad. But, in that case, no attempt should be made so sharply to differentiate the ballad in origins from other types of lyric verse. Those scholars who hold both positions at the same time, affirming that ballads originated as dance songs, yet that they were manifestly composed in some way utterly different from other lyric verse, are maintaining positions which are incompatible.

To the present writer, the gift of song seems as instinc-tive in man as the gift of rhythmic motion, not a develop-ment from the latter. Both were his from the first. No festal dancing chorus of a unanimous throng is needed to account for the song of birds, and song, the expression of emotion, not motion, may well be as instinctive in man as in birds. Other lyric forms, as lullabies, conjuring or healing songs, labor songs, love songs, are as primitive as choral dance songs, not offshoots of the latter. Children sing instinctively, and they make their own songs, with-out waiting for the communal inspiration of group danc-ing; and it is commonly assumed that the development of the child mirrors that of the race. The beliefs that from the dance emerged music and rhythmical utterance, or song, that dance songs are the earliest lyrics, that narrative songs are the earliest dance songs, and that the English ballad type had its genesis in the dance, are neither borne out by the evidence, nor intrinsically probable.

CHAPTER III

BALLADS AND THE ILLITERATE

" A ballad," says F. Sidgwick, " is, and always has
been, so far from being a literary form that it is in its
essentials not literary, and it, we shall see, has no single
form. It is of a *genre* not only older than the Epic, older
than Tragedy, but older than literature, older than the
alphabet. It is *lore,* and belongs to the illiterate." [1]
" You cannot write a popular ballad; in truth you cannot
even write it down. At best you can but record a number
of variants, and in the act of writing each one down you
must remember that you are helping to kill that ballad."
Professor Gummere speaks of " The homogeneous and
unlettered state of the ballad-makers " and remarks that
" Indeed, paper and ink, the agents of preservation in the
case of ordinary verse, are for ballads the agents of de-
struction." [2] Professor Charles S. Baldwin refers to
" unrecorded tales; tales not written but sung; tales com-
posed, not for gentlefolk, but for the common unlettered
people. These are the ballads." " Beginning in what-
ever way among the common people," he continues, " they
were cherished, circulated, and handed down among the
common people." [3]

[1] *The Ballad,* pp. 7, 39.
[2] *The Popular Ballad,* and " Ballads " in *A Library of the World's
Best Literature.*
[3] *English Mediæval Literature,* pp. 242, 331.

When contemporary English and American scholars speak of " ballads " they have reference to narrative songs of the character of those included by Professor F. J. Child in his *English and Scottish Popular Ballads.* Although Professor Child's name, " popular " ballads, is much the safer name, it is customary to speak of the pieces in his collection as " traditional " ballads, and to think of oral preservation as a test of their inclusion. In fact, it is pretty widely customary at the present time to exaggerate the part played by oral tradition in preserving these pieces, to endow it, as it were, with a monopoly which it should not have, and to be over-insistent upon the association of them with the illiterate. In consequence, it is also customary to speak with misleading certainty as to their origins, and as to the humble and unlettered character of the audience to whom they were addressed, and to place emphasis upon their total lack of literary quality.

It may be well as a corrective to re-examine some of their characteristics. Let us look first at the sources of their recovery, recalling as a preliminary a few more of the accepted generalizations. " The important fact of ballad transmission," says Professor Walter Morris Hart, " is their singing or recitation from memory by people who do not read or write." [4] " Our typical ballads," says Professor G. H. Stempel, " have come to us pretty straight from unlettered people living in out of the way places, people of no converse with literature." [5] Or, to quote from Professor Gummere,-" The ballad . . . is a narrative lyric handed down from generation to generation of a homogeneous and unlettered community,"; and " . . .

[4] *English Popular Ballads* (1916), p. 47.
[5] *A Book of Ballads* (1917), p. xxiii.

Oral transmission, the test of the ballad, is, of course, nowhere possible save in an unlettered community." [6]

I — SOURCES OF RECOVERY

Some of Professor Child's texts have been recovered from oral tradition of the eighteenth and nineteenth centuries in England and Scotland. Yet a surprising number, in fact, the majority of the best texts, have not come from oral sources. They have been preserved in books, or printed sheets, or manuscripts. Some of his most valuable sources for ballads were the *Pepys Manuscript* and the *Percy Manuscript;* and neither Pepys nor Percy cared only for oral sources, or even mainly for them, when they were gathering their pieces together. Professor Child, like his predecessors, drew also upon Elizabethan and later song-books, or *Garlands,* and he derived a large number of his texts from printed broadsides. In much the same way, in contemporary collections of folk-songs, made in our own country, some of the best " finds " have come from manuscript books, into which, like the Elizabethan song-lovers, the owners copied their favorite pieces. Such transcriptions have helped to preserve innumerable valuable texts. Contrary to the belief of many leading scholars, reduction to print does not " kill " good ballads, but helps to keep them alive. Insistence upon oral transmission, as an essential for their inclusion, would have barred a majority of Professor Child's best texts. It is hardly exaggeration to affirm that the most effective texts in the Child collection are those which have least claim to oral transmission.

[6] *The Popular Ballad,* p. 13; " Ballads " in *Library of the World's Best Literature,* II, p. 1307.

Even when typical ballads have been recovered from oral tradition, such recovery is not usually from the most unlettered or even from people of average gifts; but rather from special individuals. More likely than not, they are those among their immèdiate circle having the most vigorous minds and the best memories — those of outstanding rather than humble personality. Every collector of folklore knows the experience of coming upon these special people and deriving from them his best texts. The celebrated Mrs. Brown of Falkland, that source *par excellence* of superior ballads, was no spokesman of a humble and homogeneous society but the daughter of an Aberdeen professor and the wife of Dr. Brown, minister of Falkland. She learned her ballads by hearing them sung by her mother or by an old maid-servant. " Mrs. Brown," says Dr. Robert Anderson in his letter to Bishop Percy, " is fond of ballad poetry, writes verses, and reads everything in the marvellous way." [7]   Mrs. Brown was far from illiterate, but it would never do to rule out her ballads from the Child collection. The gap would be great. Even had Mrs. Brown somehow derived her songs ultimately from the peasantry, the likelihood would remain that they were not songs originating among the peasantry and carried over the borders of some local community to pass down from generation to generation. They were probably the popular songs, mediæval in style, of a period long antecedent,

[7] John Nichols, *Illustrations of the Literary History of the Eighteenth Century*, vol. vii. (1848), pp. 88–90.

The body of Danish ballads, collected by Grundtvig, comes mostly from the manuscripts of noble Danish ladies of the sixteenth and seventeenth centuries, who wrote them down as they were current in aristocratic usage. Though less cultured than Mrs. Brown, these ladies were far from humble and illiterate.

forgotten in their original homes and lingering in her day only in the byways. In general, the fact that songs have been preserved in remote districts and among the humble, is no proof that they were composed in such places and by such people, spreading from local improvisation into wider currency; but it is rather proof of the contrary. The popular songs for entertainment in social centres, the current songs of upper life, or of the main population, soon fade from the knowledge of the audiences which knew them first, to be replaced by those of later composition. At the point of emergence for popular song, lateness is an asset. But by the time that new songs have won currency on the stage, or in the city, or let us say, in the castle, or the market-place, or the ale-house, or the fair — the old have found their way into remote places and are likely to persist there, especially among that more fixed and sheltered element of the population, the women. As for the crude pieces that the " people " sometimes improvise — not very often or very characteristically at that [8] — they lack memorable quality except as they borrow from or are based upon better pieces; and they lack impetus for, and modes of, diffusion. Where something of the kind may be studied now, in existing society, observation shows that such pieces, whether composed by cowboys or ranchmen or lumbermen or negroes, or in social gatherings of the more sophisticated, are those which are soonest to die. Certainly the songs which are most vigorous among such peoples are those reaching them in some other way, with a pedigree of bygone vogue behind them. The real songs emerging from the unlettered are too crude, ungram-

[8] Usually they are very short, and often some kind of personal satire or lampoon, and are based on some familiar model.

matical, fragmentary, uninteresting to attract any one but the student of folk-song. And usually he, too, passes them by; for mostly he is stalking or seeking to salvage pieces of older style and obviously pedigreed.

To bring up a few examples, when we first hear of *Barbara Allen,* it is a stage song, liked by Samuel Pepys: " In perfect pleasure I was to hear her [Mrs. Knipps, an actress] sing her little Scotch song of *Barbara Allen."* A hundred years later, Goldsmith heard it from " our old dairymaid." Today, if we are to hear some of the popular songs, sentimental or martial, romantic or political of the Civil War, we are more likely to come upon them among villagers, surviving in remote and conservative communities, than we are in the circles which knew them first. *After the Ball* was a popular stage song in the 1890's. It is still vigorous in village communities and on western ranches, though it long ago died out in the city parlor and on the stage. The sentimental *Lorena,* which had tremendous vogue in the middle decades of the nineteenth century, lingers as a favorite song among mid-western cowboys. One of the ballads in Fletcher's *Knight of the Burning Pestle, There was a Romish Lady, of Paris properly,* can be identified as the ancestor of a but slightly mutilated, authorless narrative in the ballad style, existing in manuscript song-books in the Central West, and having faint currency elsewhere.

It is to be expected surely that an older type of English song, mediæval in style,— replaced by another style and another set of characters after the advent of printing and the break-up of mediæval conditions,— should linger among nursemaids and " ancient dames," among the spinners, pipers, shepherds, and weavers of remoter communities, often with singular fidelity of text. But it should not be taken as evidence that those from whom they are recovered were either the creators or the inspirers of them.

It is surprising that this should need emphasis; but in general, the process in literature, as in language, in games, in social usages and often in manner of garb, is likely to be a downward process, from the higher to the lower, rather than one of ascent from lower to higher. Here are some random illustrations. The game of " tag " now lingering only among children, was according to W. W. Newell the diversion of maids of honor in the days of Elizabeth; and similarly, the knightly practice of holding tournaments now survives only in the game usage of children. Pepys's stage song of *Barbara Allen* was used sometimes as a play-party song early in the nineteenth century in New England. *The Maid Freed from the Gallows* has been used in children's games. On the whole the best examples of the sinking from higher to lower may be seen in the texts of the ballads themselves.[9] Lord Randal has become in America, Jimmy Randall, Johnny Randall, Jimmy Ramble, Jimmy Randolph, and the like; he has sunk to the social class of those who sing of him.[10] The Two Brothers, Sir John and Sir Hugh, of the Scotch ballad have passed, in some American versions, into two little Western schoolboys. The game song *Here Comes Three Dukes A-Roving* has become in the Central West, *Here Comes Three Ducks A-Roving*. To pass to an

[9] The contrary process, bringing improvement, is very rare. An example is Mr. C. J. Sharp's text of the American negro ballad *John Hardy*, improved by incorporating some stanzas from *The Lass of Roch Royal*. See also J. H. Cox, *John Hardy*, in *The Journal of American Folk-Lore*, vol. XXXII, p. 505. 1919.

[10] See pp. 122, 196.

illustration from language, the pronoun *you,* the plural of *thou,* had its origin, when applied to one person, in the usage of the Roman Emperors, who liked to be addressed as counting for more than one human being. Then it became a courtesy-form in the usage of aristocratic Europe. In English speech, it has now been generalized for all classes, even the humblest, and the old singular has disappeared from the everyday language. But no one who addresses a single person as *you* recalls the Roman Emperors, or the aristocrats of Europe from whom this usage is derived.[11]

It forces the plausibilities to assume that village throngs evolved the type exemplified by pieces like *Lord Thomas and Fair Annet, King Estmere, Lord Lovel, Marie Hamilton, Lady Isabel, Lady Maisry,* and all the other ballads,

[11] Some further examples of the same process are easily cited. Riddles were a highly literary type of literature in the Old English period; compare the *Ænigmata* of Aldhelm (following Symposius), Taetwine, and Eusebius, and those in the vernacular preserved in the *Exeter Book.* In Middle English, riddling has lost vogue in higher literature but appears in ballads. The Cupids and Venuses and pierced hearts of the mediæval and renaissance amourists now linger almost exclusively in popular valentines. A Maypole song, forgotten elsewhere, survives in the ring-games of Georgia negroes (Loraine Darby in *Journal of American Folk-Lore,* xxx, 1917). Literary animal-tales, as of the frog and the mouse, were common in the fourteenth and fifteenth centuries. A song, "The moste strange weddinge of the Frogge and the Mouse," was entered in the Stationers' Register in 1580; and the words and music of such a song have come down to us. "The froggie came to the mill door" was sung on the Edinburgh stage in the eighteenth century, according to J. A. H. Murray in his edition of *The Complaynt of Scotland.* "The Frog's Courtship," by the twentieth century, survives only as a nursery song.

Perhaps more significant is the oft-expatiated-upon fact that the *débris* of pagan religions is found in folk-lore and literature alike.

appropriate in feudal castles, of kings and lords and ladies and their adventures; but it is wholly plausible and the development is easily paralleled if we assume the contrary process, of descent from higher usage to the peasantry, not of ascent from the peasantry to the aristocracy. Yet let it be said once more that the number of texts actually recovered from the peasantry, not from a more lettered source, is customarily exaggerated. In practice, whatever the theories upheld, oral tradition among the humble has never been made an essential for the inclusion of a text among collections of popular song. It has been made no such essential, for example, as anonymity of authorship or as traces of a mediæval style. Nor, in practice, has recovery from among the unlettered, rather than from some higher or written source, been made an essential for the classification of a narrative song as a popular ballad.

II.— AUDIENCE AND AUTHORSHIP AS MIRRORED IN THE BALLADS

Special emphasis is often placed upon the social solidarity of the period from which the popular ballads emerged. Professor F. J. Child had in mind the English and Scottish ballads when he wrote, " The condition of society in which a truly national or popular poetry appears explains the character of such poetry. It is a condition in which the people are not divided by political organization and book culture into markedly distinct classes, in which, consequently there is such community of ideas and feelings that the whole people form one individual." [12] Said Professor Henry Beers, " We have to do here with the

12 Article " Ballads " in *Johnson's Cyclopaedia.*

folk-song, the *traditional* ballad, product of the people at a time when the people was homogeneous and the separation between lettered and unlettered classes had not yet taken place." [13] " This homogeneous character of the ballad-making folk, by the way, is enough to explain the high rank of most personages in the ballads — princes, knights, and so on," said Professor Gummere.[14] Elsewhere he remarked more specifically, " Those high-born people who figure in traditional ballads — Childe Waters, Lady Maisry, and the rest — do not require us to assume composition in aristocratic circles; for the lower classes of the people in the ballad days had no separate literature, and a ballad of the folk belonged to the community as a whole. The same habit of thought, the same standard of action, rules alike the noble and his meanest retainer."

The unmistakable fact is that, judging from the ballads themselves, they were composed primarily for the delectation of the upper classes. The difficulty with the view set forth in the various quotations just cited is that the conditions which they assume do not fit anywhere, at any stage, in the chronology of society. The generalization is not made of primitive peoples, among whom, contrary to the usual view of literary historians, composition is not characteristically " communal " but individual,[15] but it

[13] *English Romanticism in the Eighteenth Century*, p. 272.

[14] Old English Ballads, Introd. p. xxvii; " Ballads " in *A Library of the World's Best Literature*, vol. III, p. 1307. To these citations may be added the opinion of Professor G. L. Kittredge, who believes that the ballads " belonged, in the first instance, to the whole people, at a time when there were no formal divisions of literate and illiterate; when the intellectual interests of all were substantially identical, from the king to the peasant." Introduction to *English and Scottish Popular Ballads*, p. xii.

[15] Compare the views of anthropologists. The institution of the

would be far truer of primitive than of mediæval society. Even for the pre-Norman period, one cannot think of the thrall or serf creating song of the same type as the court *scop* or the noble. If Gurth in *Ivanhoe* sang songs, they would not be of the same character as those of Richard Cœur-de-Lion. There *was* no period when " in a common atmosphere of ignorance, so far as book-lore is concerned, one habit of thought and one standard of action animate every member from prince to ploughboy." Try to imagine Jack Straw's " menye " ruled by the same habit of thought as Chaucer's Squire, or Froissart's Jacquerie by the same standard of action as Froissart himself. Chaucer knows his contemporary society too well to place the same quality of matter in the mouths of his higher and his lower characters. The interests and the tastes of the mediæval nobility and the mediæval peasantry were no more identical than were their occupations or their costumes or their destinies in general.

Songs of the adventures of the nobly born, of the deeds of the men of noble houses, were not addressed primarily to throngs of the rural variety, nor were they evolved by such throngs — not even the songs of Robin Hood, for whom the ballads claim noble descent, or whom some of them picture as an outlawed noble. In our earliest reference to him he is placed alongside Randolph, Earl of Chester.[16]

bard appears in all the earliest Indo-European literatures. There must have been (one would conjecture) *ur*-Aryan bards. If so, there is here a strong argument for high-born literary tradition.

[16] *Piers Plowman*, B text:

" I cannot perfectly my paternoster, as the priest it singeth,

But I can rhymes of Robin Hood and Randolph, Earl of Chester."
Whether these " rhymes " were or were not ballads, or ballads of the Child type, it is impossible to determine.

The very formula of introduction, used in the *Geste,* " Lyth
and listen, *gentlemen,"* suggests that his adventures orig-
inally entertained the higher not the lower classes.   *Robin
Hood Newly Revived* calls upon " gentlemen . . . in this
bower " to listen.   Robin is as " courteous " as a knight
errant.   " So curteyse as outlawe as he was one " was
never found, says the *Geste,* and he is as devoted to " our
lady " as the most chivalrous knight.[17]   But most of the
ballads have much more of the aristocratic in them than do
the ballads of Robin Hood.   Where we have the genuine
improvisations of the unlettered, they deal always with
themselves, or with happenings of near interest, in their
own region, or involving their own circle, not with the
interests and adventures and experiences of a widely
severed class — the governing class.[18]   If the peasant
throngs of the Middle Ages improvised songs we can
imagine pretty well the crude character of their impro-
visations, and their themes.   They did not concern the
love affairs of the nobly born, and knightly doings in
hall and bower.   Nor did they concern the exploits of
nobles.   It is known that the great houses of mediæval
England and Scotland kept their own hereditary family
bards, who composed pieces to be recited or sung, not for
existence in written form, and their themes were the feats
of their clan or of the noble houses with which they were

[17] In any case, it will hardly do to speak of the Robin Hood cycle
as " confined to humble tradition and the interest of a class "
(Gummere, *The Popular Ballad,* 271).   And alongside the Robin
Hood ballads, telling of archery, we should recall Ascham's *Toxo-
philus,* celebrating archery, in its decay, for the upper classes, in
prose.

[18] See pp. 153–161.

connected. Professor Firth is probably right [19] when he thinks he detects fragments remaining of several cycles — a cycle about the Percys, as the first ballad of Chevy Chase, about the Stanleys, as *The Rose of England,* and about the Howards, as *Flodden Field* and *Sir Andrew Barton.* Such a mode of composition would account, too, for the vitality of these pieces, as well as for their quality. If the men-at-arms of the Borderers made their own songs to celebrate their deeds, as Professor Gummere thinks,[20] their " communal " songs would have had little chance of preservation beside the popular songs, for oral destination, of the bards employed for that purpose, repeated by them on notable occasions and becoming traditional.

The social atmosphere of the ballads is the atmosphere of the upper classes. Certainly no peasant audience or authorship is mirrored in them.[21] The picture we get from them is a picture of the life of chivalry, not of the

[19] C. H. Firth, *The Ballad History of the Reigns of the Later Tudors,* Transactions of the Royal Historical Society, 3d series, vol. III, London, 1909.

[20] *The Cambridge History of English Literature,* II, ch. xvii, p. 453; also *The Popular Ballad,* p. 250.

[21] The earliest reference to *The Fair Flower of Northumberland* mentions it as sung before the *King* and the *Queen.* According to Thomas Deloney (Reprint by R. Sievers, *Palaestra,* XXV, 1904, *Historie of Jno. Winchcomb,* p. 195), to whom we owe our earliest text, maidens " in dulcet manner chanted out this song, two of them singing the ditty and all the rest bearing the burden." Seven versions of the ballad have survived in all, but that given by Deloney is the only one that is early. It is also unquestionably the best version. Ophelia's songs in *Hamlet* are of ballad quality, another evidence of the aristocratic currency and acceptability of ballads in the age of Elizabeth. The popularity of Danish ballads in the highest circles is well known, and when they were first printed it was through the favor of the Queen.

doings of the common people; such as we have, for example, from genuinely " communal " ranch or lumberman or cowboy or fisherman or negro songs today.   And the same composers who made heroic and historical narratives for their masculine hearers might well have made romantic and other pieces, on familiar or novel themes, for the delectation of their nobly-born women hearers, or of mixed audiences.   Such songs were short, or fairly short, of a type suited for oral recital or for singing or memorizing.   The English and Scottish ballads seem to have affiliations with classical narratives, mediæval romances, scriptural matter, and lives of saints.   There are also many plots which, as Professor Ker points out,[22] could have existed only as ballad plots; it is as ballads that they seem to have been created, and it is as ballads that they are memorable. Some of them might have been utilized occasionally as dance songs; but if so, this was not typical, and it was not an essential of their composition.

The lowly, as over against the aristocrats, hardly play any part in the English and Scottish ballads; and the ballads which do show non-aristocratic characters are those which would be least missed, if eliminated.   One mentions a hostler.   Thomas Potts is a serving-man, in the seventeenth century ballad of that name, but he weds a lord's daughter, and is himself ennobled.   The Kitchie Boy, who is the hero of another, also weds a lady of noble birth, in a ballad which is a late adaptation of *King Horn.*   Lamkin in the ballad of that name is a mason.   Add Richie Story, who marries a footman, although herself an aristocrat, and the list is about exhausted.   All are late pieces. . The

[22] *On the History of the Ballads: 1100–1500, Proceedings of the British Academy,* vol. IV.

ballads, in due time, like fiction and the drama, were sub-
jected to democratization of characters.   Later British
balladry stays no longer by the nobly-born for its heroes
and heroines.   Among mediæval types of literature the
ballad of the Child type was a type which lasted well, but
it too finally yielded to later melodies and styles, with
other characters and plots.   The personages and the stories
of mediæval ballads constitute evidence enough that the
" people " did not improvise them, for the songs which the
people do improvise, when they can be certainly deter-
mined, do not incline to be narratives, and they reflect the
immediate horizons of their makers and the limitations of
their expression.   Folk-throngs cannot produce real narra-
tives, even today, nor do primitive throngs.   There is no
instance recorded where a collaborating folk-throng or a
primitive throng, for that matter, has produced a memor-
able song-story.   Crude songs, at most pieces of tales
rather than tales, are the best they can create.   The power
to convey a complete story comes late, not at the beginning
of lyric art.

The English and Scottish ballads are not so wholly
impersonal as one is often assured.   The ballad " I " may
not often refer to the individuality of the author, but the
" I " of the singer or reciter is frequently present.   That
the majority of the ballads should be impersonal, however,
is normal enough, when one considers the purpose for
which they were created and the occasions of their delivery.
In such poetry everywhere, the singer avoids asserting his
own peculiarities and tastes.   The epic narratives of the
Old English *scopas* were not personal.   Sir Walter Scott's
folk-lyrics, tribal, marching, and elegiac, are not the work
of a clan, though they sound like it, nor are Kipling's *Bar-*

rack Room Ballads, nor our national songs, though they exhibit their authors no more than do the ballads. Why should *The Battle of Otterbourne* or *The Wife of Usher's Well* or *Sir Patrick Spens* show subjective qualities or parade their composers?   " Nine-tenths of secular music and literature," says E. K. Chambers, " did have its origin in minstrelsy," [23] and the ballads are hardly likely to be an exception.   There are references enough to minstrelsy in the pieces themselves.   The harper and the minstrel appear in many ballads, while the rustics and villagers and unlettered, from whom we are supposed to derive them, appear not at all.

A look at some of the introductory stanzas of the ballads points to progress toward, not away from, democracy, and the stages of progress are quite parallel to those of literature proper.   How the thirteenth and fourteenth-century " rimes " of Robin Hood opened, we do not know, though we can, guess.   A fairly old opening is this, of *Robin Hood and the Shepherd* : [24]

> " All gentlemen and yeomen good,
>   I wish you to draw near."

A stock opening of popular songs in the seventeenth century addresses " gallants,"—

> " Come all you brave gallants and listen awhile."

The stage of complete democratization is reached in the English and Irish " Come-all-ye's," as they are often called, of the eighteenth and nineteenth centuries.

[23] *The Mediæval Stage.* I, iii and iv. 1903.
[24] Introductions of this type seem to point to an inferior addressing superiors — hence to minstrel composition; as the vaudeville *conteur* today addresses " ladies and gentlemen."

To return from the matter of audience to the matter of
authorship, the minstrel theory was held by all the early
critics, those nearest to the time when ballads were at
their height, and when their history was fresher; and few
of the texts are older than the seventeenth or last part of
the sixteenth century.   The reference is probably to broad-
side writers when Nicholas Rowe in the Prologue to *Jane
Shore,* 1713, wrote:

> "Let no nice tastes despise the hapless dame
> Because recording ballads chant her name.
> Those venerable ancient song enditers
> Soared many a pitch above our modern writers."

But his statement concerning the superiority of the earlier
over the later balladists is true enough.   Allan Ramsay,
whose *Evergreen* has been a source of many " genuine "
ballads, uses for his sub-title " Scots poems wrote by the
ingenious before 1600," implying his belief in individual
authorship.   Percy and all the Scotch ballad collectors
held the minstrel theory.   Percy had to subject some of
his earlier views to revision, after the criticisms of Ritson;
the position between Percy's and Ritson's is the right one,
says E. K. Chambers, when writing of the minstrel.   Sir
Walter Scott, a pretty good antiquary, and nearer to sources
of supply, in time and place, than our modern theorists,
believed in minstrel authorship.   Even Professor Child
felt that " the ballad is not originally the product or the
property of the common order of people."   He states that
the ballad is " at its best when it is early caught and fixed
in print."   He has nothing to say of the origin of ballads
in dances or festal throngs, and he does not " rule the
minstrel out of court " but allows the inference that ballads

were the work of a fraternity whose business it was to pro-
vide tales and songs for the amusement of all ranks of
society.[25]   He refers often to the minstrel.   The character
and the standing of minstrels changed after the introduc-
tion of printing and the disappearance of mediæval condi-
tions.   The mediæval form of minstrelsy broke up in the
fifteenth and sixteenth centuries.   In general, there were
many types of minstrels, higher and lower.   Some recited
the poetry of others, but they themselves composed pieces
of many kinds.   There were many types of occasions at
which they sang, many types of audiences, and many
themes.   The evidence, so final to Professor Kittredge,
of [26] what they were like in the seventeenth and eighteenth
centuries, when they were in their decay, no more shows
what any one class of them produced earlier, than the stand-
ing of dramatists in the seventeenth century shows what
their standing was in the sixteenth; or than seventeenth-
century songs in general or fiction or drama show the char-
acter and quality of mediæval song or fiction or drama.
Grant that minstrels were the authors of any proportion of
the ballads admitted by Professor Child into his collection,
and it is an admission that there is no fundamental distinc-
tion plainly differentiating the " true " ballad, in origin
and style, from other types of ballads and songs.   As we
have them, the ballads had many origins, and they show in
subject-matter affiliations with many varieties of oral
recital or songs adapted for popular entertainment.

One important distinction must be borne in mind, how-

25 W. M. Hart, *Professor Child and the Ballad*, Publications of
the Modern Language Association of America, vol. xxi., 1906, pp. 757,
764, etc.

26 Introduction to *English and Scottish Popular Ballads*, p. xxiii.

ever; and it is hard to see why it has not been pointed out many times by students of folk-song, to the clearing-up of much confusion. The songs which impress the folk and find vitality among them are not the uninteresting and nearly negligible kind of thing which they are able to produce themselves. Popular poetry likes to remember the extraordinary, not the near at hand — though it may make over the remote till it seems near at hand — and the unusual not the usual person.[27] It keeps alive songs of Robin Hood, of the Percy and the Douglas, of Captain Kidd, of Jesse James, John Brown, or Casey Jones. It likes the strange, the sensational, the tragic, or at the other extreme, the comic; and it keeps alive the striking melody or the memorable refrain though it cannot itself produce these. In the nineteenth century, when popular fiction makers sought to provide a special kind of folk reading, such, for example, as *The Fireside Companion* furnished, they chose nobles and millionaires for their heroes, and made them live melodrama. They did not garb them in ordinary clothes but in silks and satins and velvets, and gave them the most thrilling adventures they could create.

[27] Compare Jeanroy, *Origines de la Poésie Lyrique en France au Moyen Age*, p. 18. " Si nous possédions encore les chansons que chantaient les bergers du moyen âge, il est certain *a priori* que ce ne serait pas la vie pastorale qui y serait décrite. Ce serait le seul exemple d'une poésie populaire peignant de parti pris les mœurs populaires. Le peuple au contraire a une préférence marquées pour les événements extraordinaires et les personnages de haut rang qui l'éloignent de sa vie de tous les jours."

It may be, however, that since all literature was aristocratic, not democratic, till the eighteenth century, nothing different should be expected, whether in folk-tales or in folk-poetry, until comparatively late. Popular songs having lower-class characters, the " vulgar ballads " of the collectors, appear in balladry when such characters begin to do so in fiction and in the drama.

But this was literature "for" not "by" the people. Their readers might not have cared for tales of commonplace people like themselves. As for the stories the people might themselves invent, these would stand no chance of popularity beside the stories provided for them and read with zest by them. If examples are needed, contrast the quality of *My Little Old Sod Shanty,* which Texas cowboys preserved but did not create,[28] with the *Old Chisholm Trail,* which they did create; or the negroes', *The Boll Weevil,* which emanated from them, with *Old Black Joe,* which they assimilated but did not compose; or the probable text of Pastor Lyngbye's improvisation of the Faroe fishermen concerning one of their number, with the "stately songs of Sigurd" which they inherited. To reiterate, for emphasis; what constitutes a people's popular song, the kind of thing which the people preserve, and the kind of thing which they are themselves able to create, are very different matters.

Let us now inquire as to the gulf between ballads and real literature.

III.— THE BALLADS AND LITERATURE

Many writers are impressed by the simplicity of the ballad language and by the want of conscious art which the

---

[28] Purely local ballads are based upon some popular model, as *The Assassination of J. B. Marcum,* upon *Jesse James,* or *Jack Combs* upon *The Dying Cowboy* (W. Aspinwall Bradley, *Song-Ballets and Devil's Ditties,* Harper's Monthly Magazine, 130, 901–914, 1915), or the Nebraska improvisation, *Joe Stecher,* on *I Didn't Raise My Boy to be a Soldier,* see p. 228. One heard during the European war many "communal improvisations" from groups of singing soldiers, such as "We'll hang Kaiser Bill to a sour apple tree," and "We'll send submarines to the bottom of the sea," heard by the present writer, both modified from *John Brown.*

ballads exhibit. " The ballad-language," says F. Sidg-
wick, " is common popular stock; the folk will have nothing
to do with the phraseology of artists." [29]   " The language
holds close to the everyday speech of the people who sang
the ballads," says Professor Stempel.[30]   Professor Gum-
mere speaks of " Such homely traditional songs as the
people sang at their village dances and over their daily
round of toil," and of "the unlettered and artless sim-
plicity which marks genuine ballads of tradition." [31]
' 'The ballads," said Professor Kittredge, " belong to the
folk; they are not the work of a limited professional class,
whether of high or low degree." [32]   Andrew Lang af-
firmed that " The whole soul of the peasant class breathes
from their burdens." [33]   Such quotations might be multi-
plied. The same note is struck in many literary histories.
Simplicity of expression and absence of artistry are to
be expected of songs emerging from and preserved by the
common people.

The crudity, or unliterary quality, of the Child pieces
has been much exaggerated; or so it seems to one who has
before him living work unmistakably of folk-composition
or adaptation. The English and Scottish ballads preserve
many characteristics pointing to a high descent, instead of
to a humble origin and gradual improvement. The evi-
dence is that their technique suffered gradual deteriora-
tion, rather than the contrary. The earlier text of *The
Hunting of the Cheviot* is superior to the later; and so
are the earlier Robin Hood ballads better than the later.

29 *The Ballad*, p. 61.
30 *A Book of Ballads* (1917), p. xxxiii.
31 *The Popular Ballad* (1907), pp. 7, 8.
32 *English and Scottish Popular Ballads*, Introd., p. xxiii.
33 Article " Ballads " in *Encyclopaedia Britannica*.

The fifteenth century text of *Riddles Wisely Expounded,* preserving its learned heading *Inter diabolus et virgo,* is superior in technique to its modern descendants and affiliations.   Another excellent illustration is afforded by *The Fair Flower of Northumberland.* It has survived to us in seven versions in all; but that given in Deloney's *The Pleasant History of John Winchcomb* is the only one that is early and it is also unquestionably the best version.

To particularize in a few points, *The Hunting of the Cheviot* has an elaborate system of alliteration, a mark of art, pointing to a professional poet, not to folk authorship.

> " Bowmen bickered upon the bent
>   With their broad arrows clear."

> " Hardier men both of hart nor hand
>   Were not in Christentie."

> " Tivydale may carp of care,
>   Northomberlond may mayke great mon."

In the later text this has disappeared.   And in the older pieces there are many echoes of the special vocabulary of the fourteenth- and fifteenth-century professional poets, words not in the vocabulary, says Dr. Bradley,[34] of every-day speakers.

> " There was no *freke* that ther would flye."
>   *Otterbourne,* 58.

> " A bolder *barn* was never born."
>   *Hunting of the Cheviot,* 14.

The favorite ballad term *byrd* or *burd,* for girl or woman, is another word which belonged to the professional poetic

[34] *Cambridge History of English Literature,* i., chap. xix.

vocabulary of Middle English, not to daily life. The stock alliterative epithets, " brown brand," " merry men," " doughty Douglas," " bold baron," " proud porter," " wan water," remind one of the " kennings," so helpful to the technique and to the memory of the Old English *scop;* also of the alliterative formulas of Langland and of the circumlocutory phrases of the poets of the age of Pope. The ballads preserve many archaic literary traits along with the emotions and culture of a vanished age. There are no set alliterative epithets or legacy-formulas or mannerisms of older aristocratic life in the improvisations of fishermen, cowboys, ranch hands, and negroes, genuinely communal and homogeneous as are the conditions under which they live.

Mrs. Brown of Falkland's texts contain literary words like *paramour,* a rhyme-word in her texts, *dolour, travail. Paynim* appears in *King Estmere* — and sounds like Percy's word. *Adieu,* hardly a folk-word, appears in *Andrew Lammie, The Gardener,* and other pieces; and *Robin Hood and the Ranger* actually begins with a reference to *Phœbus.* The first line of *Robin and Gandeleyn,* the text of which is one of the earliest ballad texts remaining, reads, " I heard the carpyng of a clerk." Traces of the retention of French accent, the language of the upper classes and the court, appear in words like *pité, forést, menyé, certáyne, chambér, contrée,* and there is frequent transference of it to native words like *lady, water, thousand,* having properly initial accent, or to names like *Douglas, London.*[35] To cite a few more points of style,

[35] Some prosodists might hold that these " wrenched accents " are only instances of " pitch accent " and derive them from Old English. Others may feel that they are merely crudenesses made

the premonitory dream (of a gryphon) is used in *Sir Aldingar,* in the way so characteristic of Old French and Middle English literature; frequent for instance in Chaucer and Langland; and many other mediæval literary conventions are reflected. There are *chanson d'aventure* openings, as in *Robin and Gandeleyn,* and *reverdi* openings, as in many of the *Robin Hood* ballads. The satirical legacy, that favorite device of the ballads, had great popularity as a literary convention in the fourteenth and fifteenth centuries.[36] The English and Scottish ballads shade off into literary and other verse of many types: *The Rose of England* into allegory, *The Geste of Robin Hood* into the epic *chanson, Sir Aldingar* into romance, *The Battle of Otterbourne* into verse chronicle. Many, like the riddle ballads, show affiliations with the debate or dialogue verse, the *estrifs* and verse contests of mediæval literature. *The Gray Cock* is an aube, *Barbara Allen's Cruelty* is nearly a pure lyric, *Johnny Campbell* is a coronach or lament for the dead, *The Holy Well* and *The Bitter Withy* are carols, and *The Carnal and the Crane* is a theological discussion in verse. It would be futile perhaps to look for some wholly unique ballad archetype, differing absolutely from other forms of verse to be recited or sung; or to insist upon emergence of " genuine " ballads from a single source, whether villagers, improvisers at folk-dances, some specific class of bards or minstrels, or from the singers of the church.

The ballads show strophe forms and basic meters of the

possible by the fact that the ballads were sung not read. But the final accent is too clearly marked, and is used too definitely and too frequently, at least in the earlier pieces, to be explained as something merely casual and fortuitous.

36 See E. C. Perrow, *The Last Will and Testament in Literature.*

types arising, it is usually thought, from the music and hymns and chorals of the mediæval church; and that such should be the case seems natural enough. The contrary process, that the people themselves should create a regular strophe, or regular strophes, with consistent meter, is not borne out by evidence or by analogy. Poetry of genuine popular creation does not know what meter is, save as it appropriates it — at that partially and inconsistently — from some model. Similarly the refrain when it is present — which is in about a fourth of the ballads — is used in the literary or art way, the way of the sophisticated. It does not resemble the crude repetitions of genuine popular creations. It is used as it is is in the *ballade,* the roundel, or the mediæval religious songs of many types, that is, in a way that is consistent and symmetrical.

Last, let us look at two ballads which have been accepted as pre-eminently characteristic, and see where they stand as regards " art." *Edward* has been called " unimpeachable " by Professor Child, " one of the most sterling of the popular ballads." It is thought by Professor W. M. Hart to show, not conscious art at all, but rather the simplest and earliest stage of ballad development which the Child pieces have preserved to us.[37] It is too familiar to need quotation in full. A few stanzas from the beginning and the close will serve to recall it.

Transactions of the Wisconsin Academy of Arts and Science. Vol. xvii.

[37] A favorite line of evolution with Professor Hart is from the simplicity and brevity of *Edward* to the epic complexity of the *Geste of Robin Hood*. Yet within the Robin Hood ballads themselves may be observed a line of decay, from the early *Geste* to the brevity and inferiority of the later pieces.

" ' Why dois your brand sae drap wi bluid,
                Edward, Edward,
Why dois your brand sae drap wi bluid,
    And why sae sad gang yee O?'
' O I hae killed my hauke sae guid,
                Mither, mither,
O I hae killed my hauke sae guid,
    And I had nae mair bot hee O.'

" ' Your haukis bluid was nevir sae reid,
                Edward, Edward,
Your haukis bluid was nevir sae reid,
    My deir son I tell thee O.'
' O I hae killed my red-roan steid,
                Mither, mither,
O I hae killed my reid-roan steid,
    That erst was sae fair and frie O. . . .'

" ' And what wul ye leive to your ain mither deir,
                Edward, Edward,
And what wul ye leive to your ain mither deir?
    My deir son, now tell me O?'
' The curse of hell frae me sall ye beir,
                Mither, mither,
The curse of hell frae me sall ye beir,
    Sic counseils ye gave to me O.' "

We may postpone, as yet, generalization concerning this
ballad, noting only its striking parallelism in structure, a
parellelism carried out to a degree that brings us face to
face with art. Repetition often aids in the avoidance
of heavy or involved construction in ballad technique, and
nowhere more than here.

The second ballad is the American text of *The Hang-
man's Tree,* of the composition of which Professor Kit-
tredge draws a sketch, .when sung for the first time by its

" improvising author. The audience are silent for the first two stanzas, and until after the first line of the third has been finished. After that they join in the song." This, many think, is the characteristic method of ballad authorship — improvisation in the presence of a sympathetic company, which may even participate in the process. When " the song has ended, the creative act of composition is finished." The author is " lost in the throng." Parenthetically, one would like to inquire what was the part played by the festal dance, insisted upon by one author,[38] in the making of this genuine ballad.

The text is short enough to be quoted in full:

> " 'Hangman, hangman, howd yo hand,
>   O howd it wide and far!
> For theer I see my feyther coomin,
>   Riding through the air.

> " 'Feyther, feyther, ha you brot me goold?
>   Ha yo paid my fee?
> Or ha yo coom to see me hung,
>   Beneath tha hangman's tree?'

> " 'I ha naw brot yo goold,
>   I ha naw paid yo fee,
> But I ha coom to see yo hung
>   Beneath the hangman's tree.'

> " 'Hangman, hangman, howd yo hand,
>   O howd it wide and far!
> For theer I see my meyther coomin,
>   Riding through the air.

---

[38] Gummere, *The Popular Ballad*, p. 117; *The Cambridge History of English Literature*, vol. II, p. 460.

" ' Meyther, meyther, ha yo brot me goold?
    Ha yo paid my fee?
  Or ha yo coom to see me hung,
    Beneath tha hangman's tree?'

" ' I ha naw brot yo goold,
    I ha naw paid yo fee,
  But I ha coom to see yo hung
    Beneath tha hangman's tree.'

" ' Hangman, hangman, howd yo hand,
    O howd it wide and far!
  For theer I see my sister coomin,
    Riding through the air.

" ' Sister, sister, ha yo brot me goold?
    Ha yo paid my fee?
  Or ha ye coom to see me hung,
    Beneath the hangman's tree?'

" ' I ha naw brot yo goold,
    I ha naw paid yo fee,
  But I ha coom to see yo hung
    Beneath tha hangman's tree.'

" ' Hangman, hangman, howd yo hand,
    O howd it wide and far!
  For theer I see my sweetheart coomin,
    Riding through the air.

" ' Sweetheart, sweetheart, ha yo brot me goold?
    Ha yo paid my fee?
  Or ha yo coom to see me hung,
    Beneath tha hangman's tree?'

" ' O I ha brot yo goold,
    And I ha paid yo fee,
  And I ha coom to take yo from
    Beneath tha hangman's tree.' "

Is not this, like *Edward,* perfect art? Neither piece could be improved, as regards cohesion, cumulative effect, economy of words, use of suspense, and climax — all of which belong to art. In general, it is students of folk-song who have given their time to backward study, not to the study of contemporary folk-song and its processes, who are able to maintain so high an opinion of the products of improvisation and of the creative ability of folk-groups; or the powers of the unlettered. Those who have dealt much with living popular poetry and its processes are less sanguine. Human ways and powers do not change very much in matters of this kind, and to the student of living folk-song, the assumption of the creation, by an improvising singer and villagers, of the lyric type of which these pieces present one of the " simplest stages," is far from favored by the evidence. Especially, the brief, consistent telling of a story, by the question and answer method, is of late, not early literary development. Genuine folk-creations know no such thing. For that matter they know no such thing as the brief and consistent telling of a *story.* There is abundant living evidence that folk-creation does not incline to the narrative song, but merely to the song. In both primitive poetry and modern communally improvised popular poetry, finished well-constructed narrative is beyond the powers of the creators of whom we have knowledge or evidence.

Place beside *Edward* or *The Hangman's Tree* a folk-improvisation by the cowboys,— surely not inferiors as poetic creators of the mediæval peasants — and the discrepancy in favor of the mediæval pieces is marked.

Since they were composed for oral purposes, for the ear not for the eye, nor for manuscript preservation, the wonder should be, no doubt, that the English and Scottish ballads exhibit so much as they do of literary quality and skilful technique. Some are inferior and some better; but they do show " art," or degrees of it; they are memorable and effective for the oral purposes for which they were intended. In form, as well as in themes and characters, they suggest a high descent. Contrast, where dates are available, early pieces with late, or American versions with their Old World parents, and make inference from the mass. The crudity and the unliterary quality increase with the lapse of time, and by popular preservation. The epic completeness and effectiveness of the Child pieces is likely to sink downward to simplicity or fragmentariness. Judging from the mass of recorded examples, there is no testimony in existent folk-song that the process was an upward process from popular simplicity and brevity to pieces of the length and quality of the *Geste of Robin Hood*.[39]

The distinction between poetry of art, which is literature, and poetry of the people, which is not, especially

[39] Professor Gummere's latest position was that the ballad is of communal origin, of dance origin, but grows more and more away from the dance-song in the direction of the epic. " Once choral, dramatic, with insistent refrain and constant improvisation, the ballad came to be a convenient form for narrative of every sort which drifted down the ways of tradition " (*Cambridge History of English Literature*, vol. II, p. 456). A song humble in origins may develop beyond its crude beginnings, subjected to the " refining and ennobling processes of tradition," or " improved by some vagrom bard " (*The Popular Ballad*, 76–79, 250). It is not till this stage of " improvement " has been reached that it becomes, in our sense, a ballad. Compare Professor Kittredge, who " rules the minstrel out of court," and maintains that he could never have created the ballads, but that genuine ballads are spoiled when they pass through his hands.

when there is insistence upon manner of origin, can be held much too rigidly and forced too far. The distinction takes care of itself if we think only of the destined audiences of the two types of poetry, and if we do not insist upon some mystical special manner of composition, under choral and festal conditions now obsolete. When we do insist upon a sharply differentiated origin for "genuine" pieces, and then try to apply such distinction consistently to any given body of folk-song, genuinely recovered from oral tradition, solid ground fails us. A definition which in itself denies to the ballad that it is a form of literature, denies it "art," and insists that it is the property of the unlettered, is a definition that is nearly useless for purposes of application. Fortunately, those who so define ballads never apply their definition in practice; just as they never in application restrict what should be termed ballads to songs that were originally dance-songs. If they applied their theories rigorously and consistently, they would have left nearly no ballads to which to apply them.[40]

It is enough to say that in English we mean by a ballad a certain type of lyrical narrative or narrative song or song-tale, which appears rather late in literary history; and we may discard as unessential for defining this type references to the origin of such pieces in the

---

[40] Professor Gummere had a way of so defining his subjects that he robbed himself of most of the material which he proposed to treat. In his article on "Folk-Song" in the Warner *Library of the World's Best Literature*, when he finished elucidating what genuine folk-song is, he had left himself no valid material for illustrating his species. He had to follow most of his examples by qualification and apology; "few of the above specimens [of folk-song] can lay claim to the title in any rigid classification."

dance — an origin rather more characteristic of other mediæval lyric types than it is of the English and Scottish song-tales — and references to their emergence from illiterate throngs. We can then call *The Wreck of the Hesperus* [41] a ballad, as well as *Sir Patrick Spens;* we can call anonymous song-tales like *King Estmere* and *Edward,* which never had any connection with the dance, ballads; and we can call Professor Child's *St. Stephen and Herod,* with its *Cristus natus est* of the eleventh line intact, or *King John and the Bishop of Canterbury,* with no marks of crudity or deterioration upon it, ballads; and we can do so with no less right than if they had been popularly transmitted and transformed.

Folk re-creation of traditional ballads, of both melodies and texts, is something that no student of them would deny. It is not the same thing as folk-origin for them, though the confusion is often made. Unlike the assumption of folk-creation, it necessitates no hypothesis endowing the unlettered with the power to create verse in uniform stanzas dignified by the consistent use of rhyme, and terse and telling and memorable in expression; no insistence upon origins in the dance; no insistence upon the superiority of the creative powers of the throng over those of the individual; and no faith in the special ability of the ignorant and the illiterate to establish a lyric type impossible for those of higher place. If folk re-creation, not folk-creation, were all that was meant when the "communal" nature of popular poetry, as over against "art" poetry, is under discussion, much controversy and ambiguity and

[41] Before it can be called a *popular* or a *folk* or *traditional* ballad, sense of the original author, or of personal proprietorship in a ballad must be lost.

confusion would have been saved.   When a piece has been popularly preserved in oral tradition and transformed thereby, the *product* is truly enough the work of and the property of the people; [42] but that does not mean that the same piece might not have been a ballad before the illiterate ever touched it in a modifying way.

[42] It is in this sense that Mr. Cecil Sharp may be called a communalist; indeed, it may fairly be said that all students of folk-song are, in this sense, communalists.

CHAPTER IV

THE BALLAD STYLE

The style of the English and Scottish ballads has often received treatment, and their appeal for the reader who is in reaction from book verse has been stressed by critics of many types. Certain conspicuous mannerisms have had attention from scholars and special students and have been utilized for special pleading. They are thought to afford ballad *differentiæ* and to throw light upon the origin of the ballad as a lyric type. That traditional ballads constitute a distinctive species is held to be due, on the evidence of stylistic mannerisms, not to their oral or sung character or to their destination as popular poetry, but rather to their origin among the folk, especially among illiterate folk.

In the following pages no attempt will be made to repeat what has been well said by others in characterization of the ballad style. Various features of it will be examined which have been brought into the foreground of discussion because they seemed pivotal. Usually the style of the ballads is analyzed without much reference to the pieces which exist alongside them in folk tradition. This is partly because of the tendency of many collectors to restrict their salvage to pieces of the Child type, ignoring or discarding many related types of song of equal or greater currency among the folk. In consequence of such specialization, the ballads are often endowed too distinctively with traits which they share with other folk-song. A study of ballads, whether mediæval or later, which does not take into account their background, tends to foster too sharply drawn distinctions or too rigid generalizations, and to make the results arrived at less dependable.

I — INCREMENTAL REPETITION AND OTHER BALLAD MANNERISMS

" Iteration," we are told, " is the chief mark of the ballad style; and the favorite form of this effective figure is what one may call incremental repetition.   The question is repeated with the answer; each increment in a series of related facts has a stanza for itself, identical save for the new fact, with the other stanzas. *Babylon* furnishes good instances of this progressive iteration." [1]   And again, " Incremental repetition is the main mark of the old ballad structure." [2]   This repetition is supposed to be bound up with derivation from the dance, as many citations will show.   " It furnishes," we are told, " the connection with that source of balladry — not of mended ballads — in improvisation and communal composition, with the singing and dancing throng, so often described by mediæval writers."   References are many to "incremental repetition, obviously related to movements of the dance "; [3] or we are assured that the ballad was " meant in the first instance for singing and connected as its name implies, with the communal dance."   By incremental rep-

---

[1] F. J. Gummere, "Ballads" in *A Library of the World's Best Literature,* vol. III, p. 1308. See also *The Popular Ballad,* pp. 117–134.

[2] "Ballads" in *The Cambridge History of English Literature,* vol. II, pp. 449, 459.

[3] *Democracy and Poetry,* p. 188.

etition is meant the ballad repetition not in the refrain way but structurally or for emphasis by which successive stanzas reveal a situation or advance the interest by successive changes of a single phrase or line. A stanza repeats a preceding one with variation but adds something to advance the story. Lyrical repetition of this type is a marked characteristic of the Child pieces, a large proportion having this structural feature. It is upon this characteristic that many scholars rest their belief that the very structure of the ballad, the type itself, rests chiefly on the dance, the communal dance of primitive or of peasant throngs. The four examples best illustrating it, those usually cited, are *Lord Randal,* first heard of in the repertory of a seventeenth-century Italian singer at Verona named Camillo; [4] *Edward,* a ballad in literary Scotch, first known from the Percy manuscript; *The Maid Freed from the Gallows,* a ballad told with perfect symmetry by the question and answer method in a version recovered in America in the nineteenth century; and *Babylon,* the earliest text of which comes from Motherwell's *Minstrelsy,* published in 1827.

As often pointed out, the date of recovery of a ballad is no sure indication of the antiquity of a ballad, or the lack of it; but it should not be left out of account when other evidence fails. The chronology of the English and Scottish ballads lends no support to the belief that incremental repetition was a characteristic of archetypal ballads or that it points to their emergence from the dance. If the

[4] Countess Martinengo-Cesaresco, *Essays on the Study of Folk-Song* (1886). "Lord Ronald in Italy," p. 214. The Della Cruscans thought of "improving" this song. The poisoning feature of the plot is more characteristic of Italian than of English story.

repetitional type is that having greatest antiquity, repetition should appear characteristically in the earliest ballads, less often in the late — those which were composed after the dance origin so often assumed ceased to condition the structure. Yet incremental repetition does not appear in our oldest ballad text, the thirteenth-century *Judas,* nor is it a normal feature of those early ballad types, the outlaw and chronicle ballads.[5] Unfortunately for the theorists who hold it to be fundamental, it appears most frequently in later texts, not earlier, and more often in the broadsides than in oral versions. It does not appear in the fifteenth-century *Inter Diabolus et Virgo,* the direct ancestor of *Riddles Wisely Expounded,* in the texts of which it does appear; so that Professor F. E. Bryant remarked, much puzzled, " it is a clear case of an early version not being nearly so ballad-like as a whole group of later ones." [6]   Says Mr. John Robert Moore, " Unfortunately . . . the facts seem to make little provision for the theory [i. e. of incremental repetition as fundamental to the ballad structure] ; for it is the simple ballads which most often have fixed refrains, and the broadsides which exhibit the most marked use of incremental repetition. Furthermore, when oral tradition adds a refrain to an original printed broadside, it is only a simple refrain without the structural device of accretion which Professor Gummere considers so characteristic." [7]   Professor H. M. Belden has pointed out that the output of the nineteenth century ballad press, accessible in the British

5 There is something like it in *Robin and Gandeleyn* and in the learned or at least sophisticated *St. Stephen and Herod.*

6 *A History of English Balladry,* 1913.

7 *The Influence of Transmission on the English Ballads, Modern Language Review,* vol. XI (1916), p. 398.

Museum, shows this structural characteristic very markedly.[8] It has been shown by Mr. Phillips Barry that iteration is a mark of the late not the earlier versions of *Young Charlotte,* whose history he has traced backward nearly a hundred years.[9] Iteration can be developed, he shows, as an effect of continuous folk-singing.

Structural repetition is not a certain test of what is and what is not a ballad and it is not to be insisted upon in definition of the type, first because it is not always present in ballads, and second, because it is as characteristic of other folk lyrics as it is of ballads. Just as a ballad can be a ballad without the presence of choral repetition or a refrain, so it can be a ballad without showing incremental repetition. The only dependable test elements in ballads are lyrical quality and a story element, and, for traditional folk-ballads, anonymity of authorship.

An excellent example of structural repetition in mediæval song other than ballads is afforded by the following satire against women:—[10]

> Herfor & therfor & therfor I came,
> And for to praysse this praty woman.
>
> Ther wer III wylly, 3 wyly ther wer,—
> A fox, a fryyr, and a woman.
>
> Ther wer 3 angry, 3 angry ther wer,—
> A wasp, a wesyll, & a woman.

[8] Review of Gummere's *The Popular Ballad, Journal of English and Germanic Philology,* vol. VIII, p. 114.

[9] *William Carter, The Bensontown Homer, Journal of American Folk-Lore,* vol. XXV, pp. 156–158.

[10] Bodleian MS. Eng. Poet. E. 1. f. 13. Percy Society, vol. LXXIII, p. 4.

> Ther wer 3 cheteryng, III cheteryng ther wer,—
> A peye, a jaye, & a woman.

> Ther wer 3 wold be betyn, 3 wold be betyn ther wer,—
> A myll, a stoke fysche, and a woman.

Or by a song on a fox and geese, which opens—[11]

> The fals fox camme unto oure croft,
> And so our gese full fast he sought;
>   With how, fox, how, etc.

> The fals fox camme unto oure stye,
> And toke our gese there by and by.

> The fals fox camme into oure yerde,
> And there he made the gese aferd.

> The fals fox camme unto oure gate,
> And toke oure gese there where they sate.

> The fals fox camme to oure halle dore,
> And shrove oure gese there in the flore, etc.

Or by this lively pastoral, which might possibly be a dance song, but which is not a ballad.[12]

> I haue XII oxen that be fayre & brown,
> & they go a grasynge down by the town;
> With hay, with howe, with hay!
> *Sawyste thow not myn oxen, you litell prety boy?*

> I haue XII oxen & they be ffayre and whight,
> & they go a grasyng down by the dike;

[11] Cambridge University Library, M. S. Ee, 1, 12. There are 18 stanzas.

[12] MS. Balliol 354. Flügel, *Anglia*, vol. XXVI, p. 197. Ed. Dyboski, E. E. T. S., Extra Series, 101 (1907), p. 104.

With hay, with howe, with hay!
Sawyste not you myn oxen, you lytyll prety boy?

I haue XII oxen & they be fayre and blak,
And they go a grasyng down by the lak;
With hay, with howe, with hay!
Sawyste not you myn oxen, you lytell prety boy?

I haue XII oxen, and they be fayre and rede,
& they go a grasyng down by the mede;
With hay, with howe, with hay!
Sawyste not you myn oxen, you lytyll prety boy?

Or by the *Song of the Incarnation* of about 1400, which is quoted in full elsewhere.[13]

Repetition and parallelism are also characteristic of that popular type of mediæval song the religious carol, like the well-known *Cherry Tree Carol,* classed by Professor Child, because of its narrative element and its currency in oral tradition, as a ballad. Other carols in ballad stave and showing very close relation to ballads — they have both structural repetition and a narrative element — are *The Holy Well,* telling of the childhood of Jesus, and *The Bitter Withy,* closely related to the preceding, perhaps as much ballad as carol. Some less ballad-like carols showing structural repetition are *The Five Joys of Christmas, Bring Us Good Ale, Born is the Babe, Out of the Blossom Sprang a Thorn, This Rose is Railed on a Ryse,* etc.[14] The following carol is not in ballad stave but shows a type of structural repetition, or parallelism:—[15]

[13] From the Sloane MS. 2593. See p. 175.

[14] Edith Rickert, *Old English Carols* (1910); Jessie L. Weston, *Old English Carols* (1911). See especially Balliol MS. 354 and Sloane MS. 2593.

[15] Hill MS., ed. Dyboski, E. E. T. S. 101 (1907), p. 7.

Make we mery in hall & bowr,
Thys tyme was born owr Savyowr.

In this tyme God hath sent
Hys own Son, to be present,
To dwell with vs in verament,
    God that ys owr Savyowr.

In this tyme that ys be-fall,
A child was born in an ox stall
& after he dyed for vs all,
    God that ys owr Savyowr.

In this tyme an angell bryght
Mete III sheperdis vpon a nyght
He bade them do a-non ryght
    To God that ys owr Saviowr.

In thys tyme now pray we
To hym that dyed for vs on tre,
On vs all to haue pytee,
    God that ys owr Saviowr.

The carol of the six rose branches, " All of a rose, a lovely rose, All of a rose I sing a song," applies the secular liking for the rose, as a poetic flower, in a poem of religious symbolism, in sequence form:—[16]

The fyrst branch was of gret myght,
That spronge on Crystmas nyght,
The streme shon over Bedlem bryght,
    That men myght se both brod and longe.

The IIde branch was of gret honowr,
That was sent from hevyn towr,
Blessyd be that fayer flowr!
    Breke it shall the fendis bondis.

[16] From the same manuscript. There are many dramatic carols or carols in the question and response form between Mary and an angel or between Mary and her son, in the Hill manuscript.

The thyrd branch wyde spred
Ther Mary lay in her bede,
The bryght strem iii kyngis lede
    To Bedlem, ther that branch thei fond.

The iiiith branch sprong in to hell,
The fendis bost for to fell,
Ther myght no sowle ther in dwell,
    Blessid be that tyme that branch gan spryng.

The vth branch was fayer in fote,
That sprong to hevyn tope & rote,
Ther to dwell & be owr bote
    & yet ys sene in priestis hondis.

The vith branch by & by,
Yt ys the v joyes of myld Mary,
Now Cryst saue all this cumpany,
    & send vs gud lyff & long.

Incremental repetition and parallelism of line structure
are especially characteristic of popular religious poetry,
in particular of revival hymns. It is well-known that
"repetition to the point of wearisomeness is a favorite
form of revival hymns." [17]   To cite illustration, the fol-
lowing song called *Weeping Mary*, recovered in the
twentieth century among the negroes, affords an example
of parallelism:

If there's any body here like Weeping Mary,
Call upon Jesus and he'll draw nigh,
He'll draw nigh.
O glory, ·glory, glory, hallelujah,
Glory be to God who rules on high.

[17] E. B. Miles, *Some Real American Music, Harper's Magazine*,
vol. 109, pp. 121–122.

> If there's anybody here like praying Samuel,
> Call upon Jesus, etc.
>
> If there's anybody here like doubting Thomas,
> Call upon Jesus, etc.

This song is thought by Mr. H. E. Krehbiel to be an original Afro-American song, and he printed it as such.[18] He limits his claim for the originality of negro songs to their religious songs, their "shouts" and "spirituals." But *Weeping Mary* can be traced to the singing of a white woman who had learned it at a Methodist protracted meeting somewhere between 1826 and 1830, long antedating its appearance among the negroes.[19] There were many stanzas of repetitional pattern and the whole might be continued indefinitely.[20] A similar history may be noted for a song included among T. P. Fenner's collection of *Religious Folk Songs of the Negro* as sung on plantations: [21]

> Wonder where is good old Daniel,
>   Way over in the Promise Lan', etc.
>
> Wonder where's dem Hebrew children, etc.
>
> Wonder where is doubtin' Thomas, etc.
>
> Wonder where is sinkin' Peter, etc.

Compare with this the old revival hymn— [22]

[18] *Afro-American Folk-Song*, 1914.
[19] See *Modern Language Notes*, vol. 33, p. 442, 1918.
[20] See note 57, p. 158.
[21] New Ed. 1909, p. 107.
[22] See "Old Revival Hymns" in *The Story of Hymns and Tunes* by Theron Brown and Hezekiah Butterworth, 1896.

> Where now where are the Hebrew children?
> They went up from the fiery furnace, etc.
>
> Where now is the good Elijah? etc.
>
> Where now is the good old Daniel? etc.

The climax was reached with

> By and by we'll go to meet him,
> By and by we'll go to meet him,
> By and by we'll go to meet him,
> Safely in the Promised Land.

It might be mentioned also that the " chariot " frequent in negro spirituals played a rôle in older revival poetry,[23] But whatever their origin, negro revival hymns and plantation songs, like the folk-songs of white people, abound in instances of structural repetition and in sequences of various types.   Three examples may be given: [24]

Save Me, Lord, Save Me

> I called to my father;
>   My father hearkened to me.
> And the last word I heard him say
>   Was, Save me, Lord, save me.
>
> I called to my mother, etc.
>
> I called to my sister, etc.
>
> I called to my brother, etc.

23 Compare H. H. Milman's popular hymn, *The Chariot of Christ*, or *The Last Day*.

24 Marshall W. Taylor, *A Collection of Revival Hymns and Plantation Melodies*, 1883.

I called to my preacher, etc.

I called to my leader, etc.

I called to my children, etc.

He Set My Soul Free

Go and call the bishops in,
Go and call the bishops in,
Go and call the bishops in,
    And ask them what the Lord has done.

Go and call the elders in, etc.

Go and call the deacons in, etc.

Go and call the leaders in, etc.

Go and call the Christians in, etc.

Resurrection of Christ

Go and tell my disciples,
Go and tell my disciples,
Go and tell my disciples,
    Jesus is risen from the dead.

Go and tell poor Mary and Martha, etc.

Go and tell poor sinking Peter, etc.

Go and tell the Roman Pilate, etc.

Go and tell the weeping mourners, etc.

Natalie Curtis Burlin's texts, though somewhat shrunken from those of the same songs in earlier collections, show the same liking for sequences:— [25]

[25] *Negro Folk-Songs*, recorded by Natalie Curtis Burlin. 1918.

> O ride on Jesus,
>   Ride on, Jesus,
>   Ride on, conquerin' King.
>   I want t'go t'Hebb'n in de mo'nin'.
>
> Ef you see my Father,
>   O yes,
>   Jes' tell him fo' me,
>   O yes,
>   For t' meet me t'morrow in Galilee:
>   Want t'go t'Hebb'n in de mo'nin'.

Following verses may substitute the words " sister " and " brother " for " mother " and " father."   A second song, of similar pattern, is this:—

> Good news, Chariot's comin',
> Good news, Chariot's comin',
> Good news, Chariot's comin',
> An' I don't want her leave-a me behin'.

> Dar's a long white robe in de Hebb'n I know, etc.

Later verses open —

> Dar's a starry crown in de Hebb'n, I know, etc.

> Dar's a golden harp in de Hebb'n, I know, etc.

> Dar's silver slippers in de Hebb'n, I know, etc.

Repetition in iterative or sequence form is also characteristic of contemporary ·student songs, as *Forty-Nine Bottles A-Hanging on the Wall,* or the *Song of a Tree* (*The Green Grass Grows All Round*), or the old-time temperance songs, like *The Tee-Totallers Are Coming,* or

The Cold-Water Pledge. And it may be a characteristic of popular laments, as *The Lyke-Wake Dirge.* It is found in nursery songs like *One, two, buckle my shoe,* or *One little, two little, three little Injuns,"* etc., and in lullabies, like many which have been preserved from the fifteenth century. Most fundamentally, it is characteristic of orally preserved game and dance songs, which have been illustrated in another chapter; but here it is of the interweaving type, is stable and part of the fabric of the song, not iteration of the type characteristic of the ballads.

Incremental repetition appears very strikingly in American folk-songs, all of British importation, in dialogue form, which are never classified as ballads. An instance is the familiar: —

> O where have you been, Billy Boy, Billy Boy?
> O where have you been, charming Billy?"
> "I have been for a wife, she's the treasure of my life,
> She's a young thing but can't leave her mother."

He is asked whether his wife can make a cherry pie, a feather bed, a loaf of bread, a "muly cow," etc., and gives humorous responses. In *The Quaker's Courtship* the wooer says in repetitional stanzas that he has a ring worth a shilling, a kitchen full of servants, a stable full of horses, etc., and asks if he must join the Presbyterians; but he meets rebuff. In *Soldier, Soldier, Won't You Marry Me?,* the soldier answers in lyrical sequences that he has no shoes to put on, then that he has no coat, then that he has no hat. When the girl has brought these, the song ends with the question —

> "How could I marry such a pretty little girl
> When I have one wife to home?"

In the familiar *The Milkmaid,* which sounds like a survival of a *pastourelle,* a maiden is asked in stanzas of the iterative type " O where are you going, my pretty maid ? " whether she may be accompanied, what her father is, and what her fortune ?   She answers that she is going milking, that her father is a farmer, that her face is her fortune, etc., and when her questioner follows this last statement by the remark " Then I won't have you, my pretty maid," she responds with " Nobody asked you," etc.   To cite a last example of these dialogue folk-songs showing incremental repetition, in *A Paper of Pins,* the wooer offers the girl a paper of pins, a little lap dog, a coach and four, a coach and six, the key of his heart, and finally a chest of gold, if she will marry him.   All the offers are refused until the last.   When this is accepted, he closes the sequence with —

" Ha, ha, money is all, woman's love is nothing at all.
I'll not marry, I'll not marry, I'll not marry you."

Farther, structural repetition is not a mannerism appearing in primitive poetry.   There is limitless and wearisome iteration and choral response, but no telling of stories by the question and answer method of *Lord Randal, Edward, The Maid Freed from the Gallows,* and *Babylon.* As for the cowboy pieces,[26] in those which their collector indicates as of communal composition, such narrative as they have is not presented by incremental repetition or by

[26] An example is afforded by *The Song of the " Metis " Trapper* by Rolette, Lomax, *Cowboy Songs,* p. 320, the stanzas of which open in sequence, " Hurrah for the great white way," " Hurrah for the snow and the ice," " Hurrah for the fire and the cold," " Hurrah for the black-haired girls," but the cowboy songs as a whole do not exhibit structural repetition.

the question and answer method but in a far less skilful or lyrical way.

The truth is that repetition, structural or stanzaic, verbal, of the refrain type, or consisting of interweaving lines, may be found in all types of popular poetry, from nursery songs to revival hymns. Old French literature is that richest in mediæval lyric poetry and in dance songs, but old French lyrics and dance songs bear no resemblance to ballads and they are plainly aristocratic. Structural iteration belongs to popular song in general, indeed it is very likely to be developed through folk-preservation when it did not belong to a song in its original form. It is not certain proof of dance origin even among primitive peoples. It characterizes not only dance lyrics but revival hymns, game and labor songs, student songs, lullabies and nursery songs, Christmas carols, laments, and songs and folk-lyrics in general. It is not a test of the ballad style, is not a ballad *differentia,* since it belongs to other styles also. And it is not a test of age for it is not present in some of the oldest ballads and is developed in late variants of newer ballads. Moreover it is a mannerism easily caught and of great assistance in promoting folk-participation in singing. The ballad is the only type of folk song showing structural repetition or parallelism of line in the presentation of *narrative,* but that is because it is the only type of folk-lyric which presents narrative. Structural repetition in ballads should not be cited as proof that the latter were composed in some manner different from other lyric verse, for it is a feature which ballads share with folk-song of many types; nor is its appearance in individual ballads proof of the antiquity in type of such ballads.

Besides incremental repetition, other ballad mannerisms which have received emphasis are the so-called " climax of relatives " and the ballad motive of the legacy, or the giving of testamentary instructions. Both are well illustrated by *The Hangman's Tree,* a text of which is quoted in full in another chapter.[27]   In neither mannerism may certainly be seen proof of antiquity or of the communal origin of a ballad. Both appear in the later rather than in the earlier ballad texts; and the climax of relatives — better called a sequence of relatives, or better still a sequence merely, for the sequence may be of persons other than relatives, or of things [28]— is, as we have just seen, a characteristic of revival poetry and of general folk poetry as well. Neither mannerism appears in *Judas,* our oldest ballad text, nor in the ballads which go back with certainty to the fifteenth century, nor in texts from the early sixteenth century. They might for balladry, if chronology of appearance count, be termed a sign of comparative lateness. And they need not be unfailing signs of communal origin. Will and testament features played an important part in mediæval literature,[29] and by the early modern period their legacy might well appear in traditional verse. Like the sequence of relatives, the giving of testamentary instructions is a mannerism easily caught and memorable, and it is in no way remarkable that it should be found in ballads, alongside the " last goodnights," riddling, and other devices of lit-

27 See p. 113.
28 See the sequence of kirks in *The Gay Goshawk,* or of harpstrings or of tunes in *The Two Sisters.*
29 E. C. Perrow, *Will and Testament Literature. Publications of the Wisconsin Academy of Sciences,* vol. XVII.

erature of the past.   The probability is that the legacy
feature of the percentage of the English and Scottish bal-
lads which show it is a literary heritage.   The rapidity
with which an easily caught mannerism may spread may
be illustrated by the " come all ye " opening of the broad-
sides, or by the assimilation of the briar-rose motive at
the end of texts of *Fair Margaret and Sweet William, Lord
Lovel, Earl Brand,* and *Barbara Allen,*[30] or of the stanzas
beginning —

> " O who will shoe your feet, my love,
>   And who will glove your hand? "

of *The Lass of Roch Royal.*   In the texts of Cecil J. Sharp
and Mrs. Campbell, these stanzas have spread to *The Re-
jected Lover,* and *The True Lover's Farewell,* and even
to *John Hardy,* which seems to have been originally a negro
song.[31]

A certain type of sequence of relatives is rather stock
in popular song of the eighteenth and nineteenth centuries,
especially in songs of the death bed or death-bed confes-
sion type.   In *The Cowboy's Lament* (*The Dying Cow-
boy*), which derives from an eighteenth century Irish
popular song,[32] the speaker asks to have messages sent
to his mother, his sister, his sweetheart.   In Caroline E.
E. Norton's *Bingen on the Rhine,* the sequence runs " Tell
my brothers and companions," " Tell my mother," " Tell
my sister," " There's another — not a sister."   *The Dy-*

---

[30] As in C. J. Sharp's text, *Folk-Song from the Southern Appala-
chians,* p. 96.

[31] *Folk-Song from the Southern Appalachians.*   See nos. 56, 61,
87.

[32] Lomax, *Cowboy Songs,* p. 74.   For its origin, see Mr. Phillips
Barry's article, cited p. 207.

ing Californian, widely known over the United States in
folk song, runs in the longest of its Nebraska variants,
" Tell my father when you meet him," " Tell my mother,"
" Tell my sister," " 'Tis my wife I speak of now," etc.   In
O Bury Me not on the Lone Prairie, as in the sea piece
which was its model, is the same sequence, mother, sister,
sweetheart, to whom messages are to be delivered.   So in
Buena Vista Battlefield,[33] messages are to be sent from the
dying soldier to father, mother, sweetheart; and in *The
Last Longhorn,* a cowboy piece patterned on this type of
poem —

An ancient long-horned bovine lay dying by the river;
There was lack of vegetation and the cold winds made him
    shiver —

are found " Tell the Durhams and the Herefords," " Tell
the coyotes," etc.   Still another example is afforded by
A Poor Lonesome Cowboy, " I ain't got no father," "I
ain't got no mother," " I ain't got no sister," " I ain't got
no brother," " I ain't got no sweetheart "—

> I'm a poor lonesome cowboy
> And a long ways from home.

All this illustrates how easily a familiar pattern, known
through some well-known song or songs, is assimilated.
None of the American pieces cited, unless the last, may
fairly be said to have had communal origin.

Various other marks of style for the English and Scot-
tish popular ballads, besides incremental repetition, the
giving of testamentary instructions, and the sequence of
relatives — for example, presenting narrative by question

[33] *Cowboy Songs,* pp. 3, 34, 197.

and answer, the ballad vocabulary, the use of set epithets, alliterative formulæ, and the like, have been treated in other chapters.

II — DIALOGUE AND SITUATION BALLADS AND THEORIES OF DEVELOPMENT

That situation ballads in dialogue form represent a primal type of ballad and that there is development from these to length and complexity is a view which is often brought forward. According to Professor Walter Morris Hart, " the ballad, in its simplest and most typical forms, might be called a short story in embryo. It is a song about a single situation " . . . " there is development from the simple to the complex, from the homogeneous to the heterogeneous . . . the simplest and most homogeneous ballads or groups of ballads are actually older or representative of something older, than the most complex and heterogeneous. We have already traced this development from the relatively simple ballad of *Edward* to the relatively complex *Gest of Robyn Hode.*" [34] An adherent of the same school formulates this theory of development as follows: " Dialogue is the primitive fact; scenario, character, and other explanatory matters come later. The older and more primitive a ballad is, generally speaking, the greater the proportion of dialogue " . . . " We can now understand what Gummere calls communal composition and can see the significance . . . of such things as refrain and dialogue. They are principles of composition. They make possible the production of a fairly well-or-

[34] *English Popular Ballads* (1916), pp. 45, 49. This is the thesis of Professor Hart's *Ballad and Epic, Harvard Studies and Notes in Philology and Literature* (1907), IX.

dered ballad by the common activity of the whole tribe." [35]

This hypothesis of development is quite unproved, and tested by the processes of living folk-song and by the songs of savage tribes, it is improbable. And an interesting feature of the assumption underlying it is its inconsistency. The writers who hold it affirm that the ballad is the earliest universal form of poetry, yet by their own theories the early simple forms only later become ballads by developing complexity and plot. The ballads are the earliest form of song, yet they develop from earlier song.

The date of recovery of ballads is not a decisive factor in determining their antiquity, yet it is to be taken into account. Judging by the date of recovery, the situation ballads, *Edward* and *Lord Randal* — from the simplicity of whose structure Professor Hart develops the epic complexity of the Robin Hood ballads — are of later rather than earlier composition. They certainly come to us in late form, as pointed out elsewhere. *Edward* is told as completely and with as telling use of suspense and climax as a literary ballad like Rossetti's *Sister Helen*. It is a somewhat doubtful evolution which passes onward from the artistic quality of these pieces into the crudeness and length of the Robin Hood narratives. But aside from the late appearance of the best ballads illustrating the " earliest " stage, it should be pointed out that in general the presence of dialogue in poetry is a sign of compara-

[35] G. H. Stempel, *A Book of Ballads* (1917), pp. xvi, xxvii. Possibly this is the view also of Professor F. M. Padelford, who speaking of the debate of holly and ivy in mediæval literature remarks that " like other songs of winter and summer, it harks back to that communal period when dialogue was just beginning to emerge from the tribal chorus." *Cambridge History of English Literature,* II, p. 431.

tive lateness in composition. It does not appear in the
epic poetry of early peoples. The speeches of characters
in Homer, Virgil, *Beowulf* are long declamations. So
in the older dramas, the speeches are long declamations.
The breaking up of the talk of characters, in narrative
and dramatic literature, into give-and-take dialogue occurs,
as it were, before our eyes. In the Old English period
there is very little in the poetical literature that could be
called dialogue. The nearest is to be found in the works
of Cynewulf and his school. It is after the Norman
Conquest that it begins to enter, in lyric and narrative
minstrelsy, until dialogue in one form or another, it is
agreed by scholars, becomes part of the minstrel's and
the song composer's stock in trade.[36] In Old French lit-
erature, so largely the source of or so largely influencing
Middle English literature, dialogue or semi-dialogue ap-
pears in *chansons à danser* of literary type between soloists
and a chorus, in *chansons à personnages,* or *chansons de mal*

[36] An excellent example of use of the question and answer method
is afforded by the early fourteenth century song of a maiden whose
food was " the primrose and the violet " and whose bower was " the
red rose and the lily flower," preserved in the MS. Rawlinson D
914 f 1. It is too properly a song to be termed " literary " but it
is obviously for sophisticated circles and of the " conscious art "
type. Middle English religious lyrics afford many examples of
dialogue songs.

There is an excellent example of a question and answer lyric,
between a mother and daughter in the ballad manner in Old Portu-
guese troubadour poetry, by King Denis (1279–1325), *Das Lieder-
buch des Königs Denis von Portugal,* ed. H. R. Lang (1894), pp.
xcv, 75; Ferdinand Wolf, *Studien zur Geschichte der Spanischen und
Portuguiesischen Nationalliteratur* (1859), p. 708. Examples may
be found also in Old Italian poetry. Dialogue between mother and
daughter, like other dialogue forms, seems to have been a popular
troubadour mode.

mariées, in *pastourelles* — all these in the form in which we have them being of minstrel origin. It appears, as so well known, in the elaborate debates, disputes, and the like, which the Middle Ages so liked. From these lyrical debates it probably entered the *ballades* in dialogue form [37] in which it remained popular for three centuries. Lyrical dialogue and question and answer are both characteristic enough of late mediæval " art " song for derivation, when they appear in the ballads, from tribal improvisation or from that of peasant communes, to be unnecessary and improbable.

It is known that mediæval minstrels often recited or gave a type of impersonation dramatically. Monologue and dialogue were rendered dramatically, though by one person. There are clear traces of this in many religious narratives and songs. Thus may have been given the early religious ballads of *Judas* and *St. Stephen and Herod.* The presence of dialogue and dramatic situation in such abundance in the ballads might well have some relation to a dramatic manner of delivery. The more song-like lyrical ballads, those with refrains, are not those preserved to us in the oldest texts but come from the Tudor period and thereafter.

Professor Hart's theory of development from the short and simple to the long and complex sounds authentic but there are many considerations which do not reinforce it. It would be easy and plausible, if we discard chronology, to build up a theory of development from the short one-act plays of the twentieth century to the five-act dramas of the Elizabethans; or from the short story of the nineteenth century to the long novel of the eighteenth; or from

[37] Helen Louise Cohen, *The Ballade* (1915), p. 56.

the periodical essays of the eighteenth to many of the longer prose types, the sermon, the oration, the treatise, the satire, which preceded it. If there is development in literature from simplicity to complexity there is also development from length and complexity to brevity and simplicity. Fair analogy may be drawn with the development in language, as illustrated by the complex inflectional structure of Sanskrit or Greek compared with the simplified analytical structure of present English. There is a linguistic tendency to shorten and simplify forms, to drop inflections, and to analyse " sentence-words " into short elements, co-existent with the tendency, earlier recognized, to lengthen monosyllables into polysyllables by composition. In the chronology of Indo-European languages, the languages of complex structure appear early and those simplest in structure come last. And this duality of development may be paralleled from literature.

The mass of the English ballads, or lyrical narratives, certainly appear in literary history later than do the epics and *chansons de geste* into which they are supposed to develop. Says E. K. Chambers, " The ballad, indeed, at least on one side of it was the *detritus* as the *lai* had been the germ of romance." [38] Professor Ker points out that " . . . it is certain that the ballads of Christendom in the Middle Ages are related in a strange way to the older epic poetry. . . . The ballad poets think in the same manner as the epic poets, and choose by preference the same kind of plot." [39] As the epic and romantic long narratives, to be recited or sung, become outworn, new lyrical narratives to be recited or sung appear. In any

[38] *The Mediæval Stage*, I, p. 69.
[39] *English Literature: Mediæval*, p. 161.

case, it is not proved that the transition was from ballad to epic in mediæval literature, from short narratives to be recited or sung to long and complex pieces to be recited or read. A case could be made out by some one caring to elaborate the thesis, for the development from mediæval epic to mediæval ballad. No material at all, if the facts of chronology be scrutinized, can be found to illustrate the hypothesis for ballad origins of a " traditional epic process working upon material made at a primitive stage not quite beneath our sight," while material illustrating the contrary chronological order, mediæval epic narrative, then mediæval ballad, exists in abundance. We are told that " even a mere comparison of early stages, in a *Babylon,* a *Maid Freed from the Gallows,* with later stages in the Robin Hood cycle, ought to place this view [of narrative development from dialogue and situation songs originating in the dance] beyond denial." [40] But the long epic narratives of Robin Hood appear early and the more song-like ones, from which the former are supposed to develop, come later. And when we watch the development of existent mediaeval dance songs, or of present-day folk-improvisations, preserved under the right conditions, we find nothing which bears out the hypothesis of development from mediaeval song to ballad, to epic. Rather is it contradicted, if we discard conjecture and stay by fact in our consideration of material.

Since both are folk-poetry and both are preserved in tradition, comparison seems especially in place between English ballads in dialogue form and game and dance songs. The chief collector of the latter, Mrs. Gomme,[41]

[40] Gummere, *The Popular Ballad,* pp. 284–285.
[41] *Dictionary of British Folk-Lore,* vol. II, p. 500.

holds that game and dance songs in dialogue form are of later origin; her opinion is based on much first-hand experience with the ways of folk-song. And it is to be noted that dialogue and situation songs appear in other lyric types beside ballads and game songs. Many carols both of the literary and of the more popular types take this form and many religious lyrics, and so do laments and dirges; and these are preserved in texts antedating those of most of the ballads.

Communal improvised folk-poetry as we can watch it among cowboys, lumbermen, negroes, European peasants, does not exhibit the ballad of situation in dialogue form telling a story. As for primitive poetry, it is rather the progenitor of modern poetry and drama in general than specifically of a dialogue (ultimately becoming an epic) ballad type [42] which makes its appearance during the Middle Ages. In neither modern improvised folk poetry nor in the choral singing and response of primitive poetry is to be found the body of material needed to bear out the theory stated at the outset of this chapter. Simple as it may seem, to tell a story with completeness and cohesion by dialogue is much too difficult for folk art, whether mediaeval, modern, or primitive. The safe generalization is that the story song is not a primary but a developed type in the evolution of literature, that the story song

[42] An illustration from primitive poetry representing the nearest approach which is reached to dialogue ballads is afforded by the harvest-song dance of a Boro chief, a two-line strophe to which his wife responds, in two lines of nearly the same words, to be followed by the same two lines from a chorus. See T. Whiffen, *The North-West Amazons* (1915), p. 199. But such songs of primitive peoples are not the special ancestor of that minor lyric type, the ballad, but of song of many kinds.

in which dialogue predominates is still later,[43] and that both emerge from a higher origin than unlettered folk-improvisation.

III — THE " UNIFORMITY " OF THE BALLAD STYLE

" It is a significant fact," says a well-known writer on ballads,[44] " that wherever found, the ballad style and manner are essentially the same." Many make the same generalization. But this is true only in the most general sense. It presupposes too great fixity in the ballad style. The ballad is a lyric type exhibiting epic, dramatic, and choral elements; but within the type there is as great variation as within other lyric types. The ballad style is hardly more " essentially the same " than the song style in general, or the sonnet style, or the ode style. There is no single dependable stylistic test even for the English and Scottish traditional ballads; and there are wide differences between the ballads of divergent peoples, Scandinavian, German, Spanish, American. There are differences in the stanza form, in the presence and use of refrains, iteration, and choral repetition, in the preservation of archaic literary touches, in the method of narration, and the like. The similarity in style of the pieces he included was the chief guide of Professor F. J. Child

[43] It may be pointed out that when a ballad is preserved in folk tradition dialogue sometimes gains prominence as the links in the narrative drop out. When only fragments of some ballad or song are remembered, these fragments are occasionally bits of dialogue. But such a tendency is not marked. In general it is what is most striking in the individual piece, a situation, event, tragic or comic crisis, striking turn of expression, sometimes the refrain only, for dance and game songs, that lingers in the memory, when the song as a whole has been lost.

[44] Walter Morris Hart, *English Popular Ballads* (1916), p. 46.

in his selections for his collection of English and Scottish ballads; yet he encountered such variety instead of essential uniformity that he was often in doubt what to include and what to omit, and fluctuated in his decisions. He made many changes of entry between his *English and Scottish Ballads,* published in 1858–1859, and his final collection published in ten parts, from 1882–1898.   He would not have altered his decision concerning so many pieces had the test of style been so dependable as is usually assumed.

Even the stanzaic structure of ballads is not uniform. Some of the older ballad texts are in couplet lines, while the later are usually in quatrains, and there are many variants of both forms.   The ballad stanza is hardly more stable than the hymn stanza.   And it varies not only in form but in movement, in the character of the expression, and in the lyrical quality.   Sometimes the story is told in the third person, sometimes, as in *Jamie Douglas,* in the first person, as is the case in so many Danish ballads. The ballads were obviously composed to be recited, or to be sung to or by popular audiences; and, like hymns, they show brevity and simplicity of form.   Otherwise there is wide fluctuation.   Were the style " essentially the same " the differences in the quality of the ballads would lie only in their plots.   Yet two texts of the same story often have a gulf between them.   A staple example may be found in the narration of the same occurrence in the earlier and the later texts of *The Hunting of the Cheviot.*   The earlier text contains the effective and often quoted stanza —

> For Wetharryngton my harte was wo,
>   that euer he slayne shulde be;

> For when both his leggis wear hewyne in to,
> yet he knylyd and fought on hys kny.

The corresponding stanza in *The Chevy Chase* sounds like
a travesty —

> For Witherington needs must I wayle
> as one in dolefull dumpes.
> For when his leggs were smitten of,
> he fought vpon his stumpes.

The same discrepancy may be noted between Percy's and
Motherwell's texts of *Edward*.

Many critics have commented upon the relative flatness
of the style of the English traditional ballads compared
to the Scottish. Professor Beers [45] thinks that the su-
periority of the Northern balladry may have been due to
the heavy settlement of Northmen in the border region.
Danish literature is especially rich in ballads. It is per-
haps due in part to Danish settlement in the North and
to the large admixture in Northern blood and dialect that
the North Countrie became *par excellence* the ballad land.
English ballads, unlike the lowland Scotch, are often flat,
garrulous, spiritless, didactic. Professor F. E. Bryant [46]
thought that the ballad of the Child type was not very
current in Southern England, where the institution of
the printed or stall ballad came to play so large a rôle
and established a current type of another and less poetical
pattern. The discrepancy in style between Northern and
Southern ballads might then be ascribed to the dom-
inance of stall balladry in London while it played no part

---

[45] *A History of English Romanticism in the Eighteenth Century*,
pp. 266, 267.

[46] *A History of English Balladry* (1913), p. 192.

in the North. Mr. T. F. Henderson [47] places emphasis
upon the superiority of Scotch lyric poetry in general in
the fifteenth and sixteenth centuries. Its "makers" and
bards were artists of special training and descent. Their
influence is dominant for generations and their legacy may
be seen in Scottish song of the eighteenth century. North-
ern vernacular song, he points out, is more closely linked
to the past than the popular minstrelsy of England. It
represents more fully the national sentiments, associa-
tions, and memories. It includes many numbers that
bear the hall-mark of an ancient and noble descent.

The relation is close of the Northern ballad style to
that of fifteenth century Scottish poetry and to Scot-
tish popular song as it emerges in the eighteenth century.
To cite illustration, Henryson's *Robyne and Makyne* and
The Bludy Sark are astonishingly ballad-like in stanzaic
form and in expression, though they were not composed
for oral currency and the themes are not heroic or border
themes. *The Bludy Sark* opens as follows: —

> This hundir yeir I hard be tald
>   Thair was a worthy king;
> Dukes, erlis, and barounis bald
>   He had at his bidding.
>
> This lord was anceanne and ald,
>   And sexty yearis couth ring;
> He had a dochter fair to fald,
>   A lusty lady ying.

The ballad mannerism of forced accent is noticeable, and
in *Robyne and Makyne* especially striking use is made of
dialogue. If these pieces had been composed for recita-

[47] *Scottish Vernacular Literature* (1898), p. 385.

tion or singing, if they had had oral currency for some generations with consequent transformations, assimilations, and re-creation, both might possibly seem the most orthodox of traditional ballads.

To return to the subject of variation of style within the Child ballads, the precariousness of style as a test of what is properly a ballad and what is not is shown by *The Nut Brown Maid*. It resembles some of the traditional ballads so closely in style as to win for itself for a long time treatment as one of the latter. It was included, for example, in the first ballad collection published by Professor Child. But it has now very properly lost such classification since it is really a debate piece, a bit of special pleading, not a lyric tale.

There are some who classify the American cowboy songs as " American ballads." [48] It need hardly be said that their style is utterly different from that of the Child pieces. Conventional epithets, wrenched accent, structural repetition in narration, use of the " legacy " motive, etc., are all missing save where the songs are made over from Old World ballads. Most, however, are songs rather than ballads, and their chief collector has so termed them.[49]

If by the statement that ballads show uniformity of style is meant that all ballads are likely to show a certain structural mannerism, *i. e.,* structural or lyrical repetition, so-called " incremental repetition," it should be pointed out that this is not a *differentia* of the ballad style, or proof of some special mode of genesis for ballads, for it is a characteristic of popular song in general. Parallel-

[48] G. H. Stempel, *A Book of Ballads* (1917), p. 145.
[49] J. A. Lomax, *Cowboy Songs* (1910).

ism of line structure and incremental repetition are found in mediæval songs, both religious and secular, and in folk-songs of many types: carols, student songs, nursery songs and lullabies, revival hymns, etc., as well as (in a distinctive way which is not the ballad way) in game and dance songs. Lyrical repetition in presenting *narrative* is found only in ballads, for the ballad is the only narrative type of folk-song; but ballads can be ballads which do not show it. Its frequent presence in English ballads is a characteristic which they share with other types of folk-song. It is not an essential characteristic of their structure, and it is more abundant in later than in earlier texts. There are many varieties of it; and primarily it is something to be associated not merely with the traditional ballad style but with the style of folk-song in general.

Comparison shows many points of difference as well as of resemblance in the styles of Danish, Russian, Spanish, Scandinavian, English and Scottish, and American ballads. What they have in common are the features on which we rest the definition of folk ballads as a lyric type. They are story pieces, they are singable or are easily recited, and their authors and origins have been lost to view. The real truth of the matter may be stated as follows. There is no universal ballad style essentially the " same " apart from locality or chronology, even when we limit our consideration to traditional folk-ballads. Within one community, however, through a certain duration, there is likely to be uniformity of style in the ballads preserved in folk-tradition. Popular preservation has a levelling effect on pieces which have commended themselves to the folk-consciousness and have been handed down in tradition. Pieces of all types and origins are made over to conform

to the horizons of the singers. A negro song may even
take on characteristics of the English and Scottish ballads
when recovered from white singers in regions where Old
World ballads play an important rôle in the folk reper-
tory.[50]   Examination of a body of folk-songs may reveal
wide divergence of provenance and, originally, of style.
Yet, as in the cowboy pieces, the appearance of homo-
geneity may soon be assumed.. They seem to be the pro-
duct of, and to mirror the life of, those from whom they
were recovered. Pieces of all types are assimilated in
folk-song; in the course of time they come to borrow ele-
ments from one another; mannerisms which are easily
caught spread; until similarity of style is approximated.
The ballad stanza, like the hymn stanza, has certain limi-
tations conditioned by the powers of the singers, or by
the vocal and psychological limitations of popular song in
general. Yet in the long run styles change for folk
poetry as they do for book poetry. British popular song
of the nineteenth century is not like that of the seven-
teenth, nor is that of the seventeenth like that of the
fifteenth. American sentimental, comic, and patriotic
popular songs of the twentieth century are of other patterns
from those current in the nineteenth. The song modes
of *John Brown, Marching through Georgia, Old Dan
Tucker, Zip Coon, Lorena,* have given way to those of
*Tipperary, Keep the Home Fires Burning, The Long
Long Trail, Over There.* These are songs not ballads, and
some of them are of British origin; but the same general-

[50] Compare *John Hardy* (Campbell and Sharp, *Folk-Song of the
Southern Appalachians,* No. 87), in which, as in several other songs
in the repertory of the singers contributing, a passage has been as-
similated from the Old-World ballad, *The Lass of Roch Royal.*

ization is true for the style of our contemporary story-songs or ballads. The uniformity of the ballad style is a uniformity for one people, or one class of people, during one or more generations; otherwise there is only the uniformity of simplicity to be expected of popular song of all types.

IV — IMPROVISATION AND FOLK-SONG

It seems clear that it is time to instil caution into our association of the primitive festal throng improvising and collaborating, and hypothetical throngs of peasants or villagers collaborating in the creation of the English and Scottish popular ballads. Primitive song and the mediæval ballads are separate phenomena, with a tremendous gulf in time and civilization between. No doubt some of the choral improvisations of savage peoples found or find permanence, as is the case with individual improvisations, and also with songs thought out in solitude — or " dreamed " in the Indian way. But such songs — consisting of a few words, or a few lines monotonously repeated — are quite a different thing from improvisations of length, having a definite narrative element, and high artistic value as poetry. Most primitive improvisations are no tax on the memory, and hardly, in view of their brevity, on the creative power.[51] A singer with a good

51 In the field of primitive ritual song there are many feats of memory that are quite wonderful. Long years are required for an Indian to become a really adept renderer of tribal rituals. See, for examples of verbal length, in the 27th Report of the Bureau of American Ethnology, the ritual song of 39 lines on p. 42, or that of 50 lines on pp. 571–572, at the bottom very nobly poetic. Similar examples are to be found in other tribes. Also there is something remotely analogous to ballad structure in such ritual songs as

voice and a turn for melody might succeed, whether he could compose words very well or not.

When it is affirmed that improvising folk-throngs created the literary type appearing in the English and Scottish ballads of the Child collection, pieces like *The Hunting of the Cheviot,* the Robin Hood pieces, *Sir Patrick Spens, Lord Randal,* etc., the affirmation is pure — and not too plausible — conjecture. We have to do with long finished narratives, obeying regular stanzaic structure, provided with rhyme, and telling a whole story — pretty completely in older versions, more reducedly in the later. To assume that ignorant uneducated people composed these, or their archetypes, having the power to do so just because they were ignorant and uneducated, finds no support in the probabilities. There is strong doubt that a " choral throng, with improvising singers, is not the chance refuge, but rather the certain origin, of the ballad as a poetic form." There is still stronger doubt of the " acknowledged aptitude of the older peasant for improvisation and spontaneous narrative song," or of a statement like this : " There can be no question, then, of the facts. Popular improvisation at the dance has been the source of certain traditional lyric narratives." [52] The following position is somewhat qualified from the preceding but it, too, represents conjecture rather than what is demonstrable : " The characteristic method of ballad authorship is improvisation in the presence of a sympathetic company which may even, at times, participate in

are given on pp. 206–242 of *The Hako.* But these ritual songs are not improvisations; nor are they of " communal " rendering.

[52] Gummere, *Cambridge History of English Literature,* II, p. 456; *Old English Ballads,* p. 312; *The Popular Ballad,* p. 25.

the process. Such a description is in general warranted by the evidence though it cannot be proved for any of the English and Scottish popular ballads." [53] The author " belonged to the folk, derived his material from popular sources, made his ballad under the inherited influence of the manner described, and gave it to the folk as soon as he had made it."

We should remind ourselves that in our day attempts to solve the problems of literary history proceed from the concrete to the theoretical. The methods of the transcendentalist yield to those of the scientist, who first gathers then scrutinizes his data. Certainly this is a better method than that which generalizes from an " inner light," looking about for whatever evidence may be found by way of support. A wise thing to do before reaching

[53] Kittredge, Introduction to *English and Scottish Ballads*, p. xvii. This view associating the origin of the English and Scottish ballads with the gathered folk-throng and improvisation has many adherents. It is the view to be found in our best known and most accessible books treating the ballads, like Professor Gummere's *The Beginnings of Poetry, The Popular Ballad*, and *Democracy and Poetry*, and it appears in the *Cambridge History of English Literature* and in the Kittredge and Sargent one-volume edition of the Child ballads, and it seems to have been accepted by F. E. Bryant, *A History of English Balladry*, 1913. Besides the many authors holding it who have been mentioned in preceding pages, it has the support of Professor G. M. Miller, *Dramatic Elements in the Popular Ballads, University of Cincinnati Studies in English* (1905), and apparently of Professor C. Alphonso Smith, *Ballads Surviving in the United States, The Musical Quarterly*, II, 116. There are dissenters from it here and there, whose work may be found in special articles. Among them was W. W. Newell, the distinguished folklorist (see *Journal of American Folk-Lore*, vol. 13, p. 113). But the theory of communal origin and emergence, with its emphasis on improvisation, retains the strategic position in literary histories and in special school editions of the ballads.

conclusions concerning the processes of the past, is to make sure what is true of the present; to look for parallel contemporary material and to keep it in mind when examining the older. If the past often casts light upon the present, the present, in its turn, may often cast light upon the past.

Surely then it is advisable, in handling problems of origin, to keep an eye upon the diffusion and establishment of types, in the folk-song of our own time, holding in mind changes and parallels in conditions, especially as compared with those surrounding the folk ballads of older times. Yet this has not been a customary angle of approach in discussions of the English and Scottish popular ballads. When considering a lyric type that arose in England in the later middle ages, critics should give it not less but rather greater weight than argument from the anthropological beginnings of poetry, which of late years has monopolized the foreground of discussion. The subjects, the authorship and composition of primitive song, and the authorship and composition of the English and Scottish popular ballads are distinct; and, for both, the affirmation of characteristic origin by communal improvisation should no longer be made.

Of late years a considerable number of pieces composed by groups of unlearned people whose community life socialized their thinking have been made available to students of folk song, namely American cowboy and lumberman songs, and negro spirituals. It is hardly likely that human ability has fallen greatly since the middle ages; yet when we see what is the best that communal composition can achieve now, and are asked to believe what it created some centuries ago, the discrepancy becomes unbelievable. The American pieces which, according to their collectors, have been communally composed, or at least emerged from the ignorant and unlettered in isolated regions, afford ample testimony in style, structure, quality, and technique to the fact that the English and Scottish popular ballads could not have been so composed, nor their type so established. In general, real communalistic or popular poetry, as we can place the finger on it, composed in the collaborating manner emphasized by Professor Gummere and Professor Kittredge, is crude, structureless, incoherent, and lacking in striking and memorable qualities.[54] Popular improvisations are too lacking in cohesion and in effective qualities, to retain identity or to achieve vitality unless in stray instances, scattered in time and place; they are too characterless to be capable of developing into a literary type like the English and Scottish ballads. There are now many collections of American folk-song, made in many States. In these collections, the pieces of memorable quality are exactly those for which folk-composition can not be claimed. The few rough improvisations which we can identify as emerging from the folk themselves — which we actually know to be the work of unlettered individuals or throngs — are those farthest from the Child ballads in their general

[54] For material in support of these generalizations, see the discussion of Balladry in America, especially the section entitled "The Southwestern Cowboy Songs and the English and Scottish Ballads." Compare further the improvisations of our own fast-dying-out ring games and play party songs (for references see pp. 61, 64), and of children's songs. For the Old World compare the improvisations of Faroe Island fishermen, of Russian cigarette girls, of the South German *Schnadahüpfln*, Böhme *Geschichte des Tanzes*, p. 239, and of labor songs, Bücher, *Arbeit und Rhythmus*, pp. 304, 327, etc.

characteristics and in their worth as poetry.[55]. Nor is
there a single instance of such an improvisation develop-
ing into a good piece, or becoming, as time goes on, any-
thing like a Child ballad, unless by direct assimilation of
passages from one of the latter. Yet they emerged from
throngs no less homogeneous, perhaps more homogeneous
than the mediæval peasants and villagers.

The most homogeneous groups in the world are doubt-
less the military groups; yet war and march songs are al-
ways appropriated, never composed by the soldiers. The
examples afforded by the war for the Union are still famil-
iar; the favorite song developed by the Cuban war [56] was
adapted from a French-Creole song; and we know the
origin of the songs popular among the soldiers in the
European war. If the "homogeneity" theory has any
value, it ought to find illustrations in army life. And do
prisoners in stripes and lock step ever invent songs?
Granting the "communal conditions" theory, our peni-
tentiaries should be veritable fountains of song and bal-
ladry. As a matter of fact, the most famous of prison
ballads is the masterpiece of an accomplished poet,—
Wilde's "Ballad of Reading Gaol."

Another thing shown by modern collections of folk-
song is that the songs preserved among the folk are nearly
certain *not* to be those composed by them. Those they
make themselves are just about the first to die.[57] Usu-

[55] It is obvious that negro songs do not tend to assume a narrative
type but retrograde to a simple repetition of phrases.

[56] Joseph T. Miles, "A Hot Time in the Old Town Tonight."
"Hail, Hail, the Gang's All Here," popular before and during the
European war, utilizes for its melody the Pirates Chorus, from Sir
Arthur Sullivan's *The Pirates of Penzance*.

[57] Illustration may be drawn also from the improvisations at the

ally some special impetus, some cause for persistence or popularity, is to be detected for the pieces that live. And the striking or memorable qualities, or the special mode of diffusion, necessary to bring vitality are just what the genuine " communal " folk-pieces do not and cannot have. Most improvised poetry dies with the occasion that brought it forth. This is by and large a dependable generalization. What the folk improvises is typically flat and inferior and has no such vitality as the material assimilated and preserved by the folk from other sources.

The test of subject-matter should also be taken into account, when we are considering the likelihood that some process akin to the processes of primitive choral song and dance — continued through untold centuries among villagers and peasants — produced the Child ballads. The real communal pieces, as we can identify them, deal with the life and the interests of the people who compose them. They do not occupy themselves with the stories and the lives of the class above them. The cowboy pieces deal with cattle trails, barrooms, broncho riding, not with the lives of ranch-owners and employers; and a negro piece deals with the boll weevil, not with the adventures of the owners of plantations. Songs well-attested as emerging from the laboring folk throngs of the Old-World deal

old time revival meetings, where " a good leader could keep a song going among a congregation or a happy group of vocalists, improvising a new start line after every stop until his memory or invention gave out." See *The Story of Hymns and Tunes*, by Theron Brown and Hezekiah Butterworth (1896), chapter vii ("Old Revival Hymns"), pp. 262–297. But these improvisations did not live or produce new hymns. The material of the revival hymns and the mannerisms of the singing, especially of improvisation and protraction, had strong influence on negro folk-song, indeed afforded the background for the negro " spirituals." See pp. 129–132.

with the interests of factory life or agricultural life, or
with the adventures of those of the social class singing or
composing the songs. The improvisations of folk singers
are usually personal, satirical, humorous, or vituperations,
are lampoons and the like, and they grow out of the imme-
diate interests or level of life or the latest occurrence
among the singers. They are not often sentimental and
are not heroic, narrative, or historical. What then must
we think of the English and Scottish ballads, if the people
composed them? Their themes are not at all of the char-
acter to be expected. They are not invariably on the
work, or on episodes in the life of the ignorant and lowly.
Would they have had so great vitality or have won such
currency if they had dealt with laborers, ploughmen,
spinners, peasants, common soldiers, rather than with
aristocrats? The typical figures in the ballads are kings
and princesses, knights and ladies,— King Estmere,
Young Beichan, Young Hunting, Lord Randal, Earl
Brand, Edward, Sir Patrick Spens, Edom o'Gordon, Lord
Thomas and Fair Annet, Lady Maisry, Proud Lady Mar-
garet, or leaders like the Percy and the Douglas. We
learn next to nothing concerning the humbler classes from
them; less than from Froissart's Chronicles, far less than
from Chaucer. The life is not that of the hut or the
village, but that of the bower and the hall. Nor is the
language parallel to that of the cowboy and negro pieces.
It has touches of professionalism, stock poetic formulae,
alliteration, often metrical sophistication. It is not
rough, flat, crude, in the earlier and undegenerated ver-
sions; instead there is much that is poetic, telling, beau-
tiful. It is for its time much nearer the poetry coming
from professional hands than might be expected from me-

diæval counterparts of *The Old Chisholm Trail* and *The Boll Weevil*.[58]   No doubt there existed analogues of these pieces, *i .e.,* songs which were sung by and were the creation of ignorant and unlettered villagers; but we may be certain that these mediæval analogues were not the Child ballads.

The English and Scottish ballads should no longer be inevitably related to primitive singing and dancing throngs, improvising and collaborating.   We can not look upon creations of such length, structure, coherence, finish, artistic value, adequacy of expression, as emerging from the communal improvisation of simple uneducated folk-throngs.   This view might serve so long as we had no clear evidence before us as to the kind of thing that the improvising folk-muse is able to create.   When we see what is the best the latter can do, under no less favorable conditions, at the present time, we remain skeptical as to the power of the mediæval rustics and villagers.   The mere fact that the mediæval throngs are supposed by many scholars to have danced while they sung, whereas modern cowboys, lumbermen, ranchmen, or negroes do not, should not have endowed the mediæval muse with such striking superiority of product.

[58] See Chapter VI, iii.

CHAPTER V

THE ENGLISH BALLADS AND THE CHURCH

Many origins have been suggested for the type of narrative song appearing in the English and Scottish traditional ballads: minstrel genesis, origin in the dance, improvisations of mediæval peasant communes, or descent from the dance songs of primitive peoples. The hypothesis of minstrel origin was that first to be advanced and it has always retained supporters. There remains a possibility not yet brought forward which deserves to be presented for what it is worth, since the problem, though it may be insoluble, has its attraction for critic and student. We have but meager knowledge of the ballad melodies of pre-Elizabethan days, and we can get but little farther with the study of the ballads by way of research into mediæval music. Moreover the earliest texts remaining to us seem to have been meant for recital rather than for singing. In general, the melodies of ballads are more shifting, less dependable, than are the texts, in the sense of the plots and the characters which the texts present. This is true of contemporary folk-songs and it was probably true earlier. One text may be sung to a variety of airs or one air may serve for many texts. Nor can we get much farther with the study of ballads by way of the minstrels. They have had much attention already; and nothing has ever been brought out really barring them from major responsibility for ballad creation and diffusion in the earlier periods. Again, we can get but little farther by studying the mediæval dance, or folk-improvisations, or the dance songs of primitive peoples, all of which have been associated with the Child ballads to an exaggerated degree. It is time to try a new angle of approach — the last remaining — although the hypothesis which it suggests is far removed from the theory of genesis enjoying the greatest acceptance at the present time, and although it — like its predecessors — may not take us very far.

It has been customary among theorizers completely to discard the chronological order of the ballad texts remaining to us, and to argue toward origin and development from a type of ballad like *Lord Randal* and *Edward,* of comparatively late appearance, when such reversal of chronology best suited the theory to be advanced. The contrary procedure, theorizing from the facts of chronology, is the logical one. If the ballad texts which are oldest are given attention and emphasis, actual fact adhered to and conjecture omitted, can anything distinctive be reached? This method of approach is one to which the ballads have never been subjected in more than a cursory way. If it is tried, in what direction does it lead?

I THE EARLIEST BALLAD TEXTS

If we accept the body of English and Scottish ballad material as defined by Professor F. J. Child, the oldest ballad texts existing have to do rather strikingly with the church. They have unmistakably an ecclesiastical stamp, and sound like an attempt to popularize Biblical history or legend. By our oldest texts are meant those

to be found in early manuscripts of established date, not
texts recovered from an oral source or found in manu-
scripts of later centuries.[1]   The earliest remaining Eng-
lish ballad is conceded to be the *Judas,* a narrative of 36
lines in rhyming couplets, which endows him with a wicked
sister, refers to his betrayal of Christ for thirty pieces of
silver, and reflects some of the curiosities of mediæval
legend concerning him.[2]   The manuscript preserving it,
in the library of Trinity College, Cambridge, is certainly
of the thirteenth century.   The same manuscript contains
A Ballad of the Twelfth Day, a ballad of the same general
nature as the *Judas* and written in the same hand.[3]   It
has probably escaped general recognition as a ballad be-
cause composed in monorhyme quatrains, a more elaborate
form, instead of in the couplets of the *Judas.*

From the fifteenth century comes *Inter Diabolus et
Virgo,* ancestor of many riddling ballads, preserved in the
Bodleian library at Oxford, a piece in which the devil is
worsted by a clever and devout maiden.   The questions
and answers reach their climax in " God's flesh is better
than bread " and " Jesus is richer than the King."   Like-
wise from the fifteenth century is *St. Stephen and Herod,*
in the Sloane manuscript of about the middle of the cen-
tury, which incorporates the widespread mediæval legend
of the cock crowing from the dish *Cristus natus est,* a leg-

1 For the dating of ballad texts, see E. Flügel, *Zur Chronologie
der englischen Balladen, Anglia,* vol. XXI, (1899), pp. 312 ff.

2 Compare P. F. Baum, " The English Ballad of Judas Iscariot,"
Publications of the Modern Language Association of America, vol.
XXXI (1916), p. 181, and " The Mediæval Legend of Judas Iscariot,"
ibid., p. 481.

3 Printed, with editorial notes, by W. W. Greg, *The Modern Lan-
guage Review,* vol. VIII, p. 64, and vol. IX (1913), p. 235.

end which appears also in the well-known carol or religious ballad, *The Carnal and the Crane*. *Als I yod on ay Mounday,* in 8-line stanzas, preserved in a fourteenth-century manuscript in the Cotton collection, is hardly a ballad, but a poem to which the later ballad, *The Wee Wee Man,* may be related. It is not admitted among ballads by Professor Child. *Thomas Rymer* is generally accounted old, since its hero is Thomas of Erceldoune; we do not have it, however, in early form, but from the eighteenth century, and there is no determining the time of its composition. There is a fifteenth-century poem, in ballad stanza, *Thomas of Erseldoune,* preserved in the Thornton manuscript, but it is usually classified as a romance or a romantic poem, never as a ballad. The existing ballad, on the same theme, is probably not a legacy from the romance but an independent creation telling the same story. Possibly it is based on the romance. Among earlier texts are left, then, only a few greenwood and outlaw pieces from no farther back than the middle of the fifteenth century. The first is *Robin and Gandeleyn,* a greenwood ballad from about 1450, which opens in the reporter's manner of so many of the *chansons d'aventure:*

> I herde the carpynge of a clerk
> Al at yone wodes ende.

Others are *Robin Hood and the Monk* (which has a *reverdi* opening), *Robin Hood and the Potter* of about 1500, and *A Gest of Robin Hood* of perhaps a few years later. There were earlier songs and rhymes, just as there were later songs and rhymes of Robin Hood,[4] but whether he was celebrated in the *ballad* manner prior to the fifteenth

---

[4] Like the "rhymes" of Robin Hood mentioned in *Piers Plowman*.

century we do not know.[5] The ecclesiastical pieces are in
the couplet form usually recognized by scholars as the
older for ballads, while *Robin and Gandelyn* and the Robin
Hood pieces are in the familiar four-line stanza which be-
came the staple ballad stanza. We should, very likely, go
somewhat earlier than the thirteenth-century *Judas* for the
genesis of the lyric type which it represents; but there is
no doubt that, in respect to chronological appearance, our
oldest ballads deal not with themes of love, romance, do-
mestic tragedy, adventure, chronicle, or even outlawry —
though the latter come as early as the fifteenth century —
but instead are strikingly ecclesiastical.

It need hardly be pointed out that this scrutiny is a
logical one to make, though it would be idle to think its
results decisive. It seems to suggest that the ballad as a
poetic type, a story given in simple lyrical or singable
form, may have received impetus from, or have been
evolved through the desire to popularize a scriptural story
or legend. In other words, it is as though the ballad, like
the religious carols and the miracle plays and a great mass
of ecclesiastical lyrics and narrative poetry, might be a

[5] The music of some of the Robin Hood songs, sometimes at least,
seems to have been church music, or music of the same type. See a
passage on "pryksong" in the Interlude of *The Four Elements*,
dated by Schelling about 1517. (Halliwell edition, *Percy Society
Publications*, 1848, pp. 50, 51.) See also *pricksong* in *The Oxford
Dictionary*. There should be nothing surprising in the singing of
ballads to music of ecclesiastical type, if such was the case. In con-
temporary folk-song, hymn tunes are constantly utilized, in the
United States and elsewhere — as in the Faroe Islands, according to
Thuren. The words of *John Brown*, in the period of the Civil War,
were put together to a popular Methodist camp-meeting tune. Jean
Beck (*La Musique des Troubadours*, Paris, 1910, pp. 19–24) leans to
the opinion that the source of troubadour music, hence of Romance
lyric poetry in general, is to be found in the music of the church.

part of that great mediæval movement to popularize for edifying reasons biblical characters and tales, a movement having its first impulse in the festival occasions of the church. Then, again like the drama, it passes from ecclesiastical hands, with edification the purpose, into secular hands, with the underlying purpose of entertainment. To follow farther the possibilities, once the type was popularized and mainly in the hands of the minstrels, as the drama passed into the control of the guilds, a variety of material was assimilated, and (still like the drama) the religious material, having historically initial place, became submerged and ultimately well-nigh lost to view. The minstrels of great houses sang of the martial deeds of those houses, as of the Percys, the Stanleys, the Howards.[6] Popular outlaws were celebrated, though in a somewhat upper-class way, in the Robin Hood pieces, in the period when outlaws were popular figures in literature; while for the entertainment of aristocratic mixed audiences, for which so many of the literary types of the Middle Ages were developed, all kinds of material, romantic and legendary and the like, were utilized. In its period of full development, the ballad shades off into many types, the epic *chanson* in *Robin Hood,* the allegory in *The Rose of England,* the verse chronicle in *The Battle of Otterbourne,* the romance in *Sir Aldingar* and *Earl Brand,* the aube in *The Gray Cock,* the lament in *Johnny Campbell,* the carol in *The Cherry Tree Carol,* and theological discussion in verse in *The Carnal and the Crane.*[7]

[6] In *The Hunting of the Cheviot; the Rose of England* and *Flodden Field; Sir Andrew Barton.*

[7] Other "literary" features of the ballads, the popular spring morning (*reverdi*) opening of the outlaw pieces and the frequent

The ecclesiastics and the minstrels, between them, were responsible for all or nearly all the new types of mediæval poetry, and (possibly enough) for the ballads too.[8]   Another illustration of the passing of an ecclesiastical mode into secular hands, is the Mary worship of the church which was secularized in Provençal poetry and crossed to England in the woman worship of the chivalric code, reflected in the romances and the romantic lyrics.

It is certain that the earliest ballad texts do not sound as though they ever had any connection with the dance. Religious material sometimes appeared in mediæval dance

chanson d'aventure opening, were mentioned in connection with the discussion of fifteenth-century texts.

[8] If ecclesiastical ballads are the earliest ballads, *The Carnal and the Crane*, a theological discussion between birds of the type liked in the Middle Ages, in which the Crane instructs her interrogator on the childhood and life of Jesus and in several apocryphal incidents, might be a ballad of earlier type than *Lord Randal*. Though itself first recorded in an eighteenth-century text, this ballad-carol has unmistakably early affiliations, as with *St. Stephen and Herod*, and early legendary matter concerning Christ. And the ballads *Dives and Lazarus*, traceable to the sixteenth century, *The Maid and the Palmer* of the Percy Manuscript, and *Brown Robin's Confession* of Buchan's collection, might represent an older type of material than *Edward* or *Babylon*. But this is purely speculative, and of no value as argument.

The ballad, *Hugh of Lincoln*, or *The Jew's Daughter*, which still has vitality, though its earliest texts come from the middle of the eighteenth century, takes us back in its tragic story and its discovery of murder by miracle to the thirteenth century. The story of Hugh of Lincoln, first appears in *The Annals of Waverley*, 1255, and in Matthew of Paris. It has parallels in the twelfth century and a cognate in Chaucer's *The Prioresse's Tale*. *Hugh of Lincoln* refers us to an old story of definite date more certainly than do most of the ballads. It deserves mention among those exhibiting, it would appear, material of older type than the outlaw, chronicle, or romantic ballads.

songs, but it was the rarest of the many types of material found in such songs.[9] There are traces of sporadic connection between the church and liturgical dancing in the Middle Ages, but established or widespread liturgical dancing is extremely doubtful. Testimonies are too abundant as to the stand taken by the mediæval church against dancing, whether by professional dancers or by the folk.

The application of the name "ballad," which means dance song, to the traditional lyric-epic did not come in a specific way until the eighteenth century; hence an etymological argument from the name, as indicating a dance origin for the species, should have no weight. A "ballad" in the fourteenth century was usually the artificial species which we now call the "ballade," a species which is to be associated with the dance. The name which we have fixed upon for them is perhaps responsible for our long association of the English and Scottish type with the dance, and for our refusal to look elsewhere for its genesis. In a manner exactly parallel, the word *carol* was applied late to religious songs of the Nativity and of Christmas (French *noëls*). When the word carol first appeared in English it meant a secular dance song of spring and love. We name religious songs of Christmas by a word that first meant dance song, as we do our traditional lyric-epics. But for the definite suggestion of their name, it might seem less surprising that our earliest ballad texts associate themselves with biblical edification, not with dancing throngs on the village green.

There are no earlier ballad documents in other countries than in England, so that the chronology of the ballad's appearance is the only certain test that we have con-

9 Böhme, *Geschichte des Tanzes* (1888), pp. 244 ff.

cerning the time of composition of a ballad text. The age of the story or theme of a ballad and the age of the ballad itself may be quite different matters. Besides, not all nations show a liking for ballads. The South African Dutch are said to have folk-tales, but no ballads. Italian folk-song, except in the extreme north, had no ballads, and French folk-song has no such wealth of ballad poetry as English has. Some parts of Spain have no ballads. The Danish ballads are those most closely related to the English. The oldest Danish manuscript collection of ballads comes from about 1550, although there are fragments of ballads and references to ballads which take us back somewhat earlier. One not very significant ballad, *Ridderen i Hjórteham,* is of about 1450. A systematic examination of Scandinavian ballads from the angle of approach of the rôle played by ecclesiastical material or by ecclesiastical agents of composition and diffusion, might have some bearing for or against the conjectures presented here; but probably it would yield little or nothing decisive. Also to be desired is an investigation of the religious narrative lyric for Old French popular verse, since the mediæval English lyric owes so much to French sources.

The *terminus a quo* for ballad origin must be the beginning of the twelfth century. Ballads of the rhyming form of the English and Scottish type cannot in origin antedate the Norman Conquest. If the Anglo-Saxons had ballads they were of the character of Old Teutonic verse, in some respects like the Brunanburh song, or the *Battle of Maldon,* or possibly like some of the *Charms;* in any case they were not in the rhyming form of the later ballads, the lyrical type which is under discussion here. The musical pliability of the lyric came from the south, across

the Channel, modifying the stubbornness of the Old North-
ern verse and its sameness of movement. Some old lore
may have been handed on into the rhymed forms, old wine
passing into new bottles, but the old song modes made
way in general for the newer. Ballads of the rhyming
Child pattern must have arisen, like modern poetry and
prosody in general, after 1100. We have one ballad,
Judas, and posssibly a second, *A Ballad of Twelfth Day,*
from the thirteenth century; and in general from 1200 on-
ward much popular verse remains. It would help if more
remained, but we need be at no loss as to what was in lyri-
cal currency or what suited the popular taste. It will not
do to assume that a type of ballad verse, the Child type,
existed among the folk long before verse of its rhyming
lyrical pattern, a new mediæval type, makes its appearance
in the lyric in general. The folk are more likely to have
adhered to the old alliterative verse with its dual move-
ment long after it had lost popularity in higher circles
than they are to have invented new rhyming forms before
these appear from professional hands.

II — SOME BALLAD AFFILIATIONS

If ballad literature began with the religious ballads of
the clericals, earlier ballads might be expected to show
affinities with miracle plays and various types of scrip-
tural and saints'-legend and other theological matter in
verse and with religious lyrics. This they do show; and
the resemblances are far stronger than they are to secular
matter coming from the same early periods. Many of
our existing Child ballads are on the border line between
ballads and carols (French *noëls*), like *The Bitter Withy,*

The Holy Well, The Cherry-Tree Carol, The Carnal and the Crane, so that they appear in illustrative collections of both types of verse. They are easily accessible in collections of both ballads and carols, are included in the Child collection, and they need not be reproduced here. They deserve either classification and make clear that the ballad and the religious carol may be related ɪorms. There is also obvious relationship to the miracle plays and their cognates. The opening and the end of the thirteenth-century *Harrowing of Hell* [10] exhibit ballad-like stanzas : —

> Alle herkneth to me nou,
> A strif wolle y tellen ou
> of ihesu ant of sathan,
> tho ihesu wes to helle ygan . . .

> in godhed tok he ·then way
> that to helle gates lay.
> The he com there tho seide he
> asse y shal nouthe telle the.

The Brome *Abraham and Isaac* is often suggestive of the ballad manner. It is familiar, and space need not be given to quotation from it. The ballads also show affinities to scriptural and saints'-legend matter in verse of narrative type.[11]

[10] Ed. all versions, W. H. Hulme, E. E. T. S., Extra Series, 100 (1907).

[11] Compare in *The Minor Pieces of the Vernon Manuscript,* vol. I, ed. Horstmann, E. E. T. S., No. 98 (1892) *The Miracles of Our Lady,* p. 138, *The Saving of Crotey City, The Child Slain by the Jews, A Jew Boy in an Oven,* etc., the opening of *The Visions of Seynt Poul wan he was rapt into Paradys,* etc.; vol. II, ed. Furnivall (1901), *Susannah, or Seemly Susan,* p. 626; and in the Sloane Manuscript 2593, *St. Nicholas and Three Maidens* and *Nowel, Mary moder cum and se,* etc. Also many pieces in MS. Balliol 354.

Among the earlier minstrels, the dramatic instinct brought impersonation in which monologue and dialogue were given dramatically, by one individual, perhaps sometimes in special costume. There are religious pieces like the thirteenth-century *Harrowing of Hell,* or like *Judas* (it may well be) or *St. Stephen and Herod,* which suggest that they were to be given dramatically. The dramatic element is strong in ballads and also in carols and in many religious poems intended to be given for instruction.

Most striking, however, is the fact that in lyrical quality and style [12] the closest affinities of the ballads of the pre-Elizabethan period seem to be with carols and with religious songs. It is in manuscripts containing religious

---

The religious tag stanzas at the end of older ballads — often dropped in later texts — account for themselves better if emerging from ecclesiastical influence than if emerging from the purely secular minstrelsy condemned for its influence by the church. Examples are the endings of *The Battle of Otterbourne* or *The Hunting of the Cheviot:*

> Now let us all for the Perssy praye
> to Jhesu most of myght,
> To bryng hys sowlle to the blysse of heven
> for he was a gentyll knight.

Or —

> Jhesue Crist our balys bete,
> and to the blys vs brynge.
> Thus was the hountyng of the Chivyat;
> God send vs alle good endyng.

But this is uncertain ground. Such passages appear in the romances, as *Sir Orpheo,* as well as in sermons, like the old Kentish sermons of the thirteenth century. In the Danish ballads, Steenstrup thinks these tag stanzas a sign of lateness.

12 The influence of the song of the early church has often been pointed out. "The lyric art, it is hardly too much to say," declares Rhys, "was in English kept alive for nearly three centuries by the hymns of the monks and lay brothers" (*Lyric Poetry* [1913], p 19).

lyrical pieces that some of the oldest ballads and the nearest approaches to ballads are found.[13]   Impose the lyrical quality of some types of carols upon a variety of narrative themes, or situation themes, and the type of ballad is reached which emerges in such abundance in the later sixteenth and earlier seventeenth centuries.   The early Tudor period was one of great musical impulse, and the singing of ballads to melodies might then have won in favor over the older recital.   Be this as it may, it is in the sixteenth century that the ballad texts which remain to us [14] first assume the lyrical refrains that both the religious and the older secular carols exhibited earlier.   The Sloane manuscript of the middle of the fifteenth century is the richest in ballads or ballad-like pieces before the Percy manuscript, and it contains mainly religious and moral songs, three in Latin, nearly one hundred with Latin refrains, and numerous Christmas carols.   The earliest approaches to the song manner of ballads which remain to us are ecclesiastical.

There is lyrical or structural repetition in the ballad manner in the early fourteenth-century *Song of the Incarnation:* — [15]

[13] The English religious lyric of the Middle Ages far exceeds in quantity that of secular verse and it appears much earlier. The thirteenth and fourteenth centuries afford many specimens. That many were written in this period is clear from the number which yet remain to us. Before the thirteenth century, most religious lyrics were in Latin.

[14] With the possible exception of *Robin and Gandeleyn*. I have not been able to see the Harvard doctorate thesis of J. H. Boynton, *Studies in the English Ballad Refrain, with a Collection of Ballad and Early Song Refrains* (1897), for the thesis remained unpublished.

[15] From the Sloane MS. 2593. And compare *A Song of Joseph and*

I syng of a mayden that is makeles;
kyng of alle kynges to here sone che ches.

he cam also stylle ther his moder was,
as dew in aprylle that fallyt on the gras.

he cam also stylle to his moderes bowr
as dew in aprille that fallyt on the flour.

he cam also stylle ther his moder lay,
as dew in aprille that fallyt on the spray.

moder & maydyn was neuer non but che;
wel may swych a lady godes moder be.

There is something of the lyrical quality of the ballads in — [16]

Adam lay y-boundyn, boundyn in a bond
fowr thousand wynter thowt he not to long
and all was for an appil, an appil that he took. . . .

and in carols like " A new yer, a new yer, a chyld was i-born," and in many others. And surely there are close ballad affinities to be found in a song like this, written down in the reign of Henry VIII : — [17]

Mary in a manuscript of the Advocate's Library, Edinburgh, dated 1372, first printed by Professor Carleton F. Brown, *Selections from Old and Middle English* (1918) ; also *Lamentacio Dolorosa* and *Lullaby to the Infant Jesus*, first printed (from the same manuscript) by Professor Brown.

[16] Bernhard Fehr, *Die Lieder der HS. Sloane* 2593, *Archiv*, vol. CIX, p. 51. Compare also some of the short religious pieces edited by Furnivall, E. E. T. S., vol. XV (1866), as *Christ Comes*, p. 259, from the Harleian MS. 7322.

[17] MS. Balliol 354. *Richard Hill's Commonplace Book*, E. E. T. S., Extra Series 101 (1907). This book contains many sacred songs and carols and many moral, didactic, and historical pieces and

Lully lulley

The faucon hath borne my make away.

He bare him up, he bare him down,
He bare him into an orchard brown.   *Lully,* etc.

In that orchard there was an hall,
Which was hanged with purpill and pall.   *Lully,* etc.

And in that hall there was a bed,
It was hanged with gold so red.   *Lully,* etc.

And in that bed there lith a knight,
His woundes bleding day and night.   *Lully,* etc.

By that bedside kneleth a may,
And she wepeth both night and day.   *Lully,* etc.

And by that bed side there stondeth a stone,
Corpus Christi wreten there on.   *Lully,* etc.

(*Lully lulley, lully lulley*
The faucon hath borne my make away.)

This song with a burden like a ballad, or like that of a
Christmas carol, was interpreted by Professor Flügel as
the story of Christ's Passion, and his interpretation was
borne out by a discovery of a modern traditional carol by
F. Sidgwick.[18]   The song is a religious song.   The ten-
dency in criticism has been to associate the ballads with
older heroic poetry or with romance, or with dance songs;
but comparison will show that, in the texts earliest to ap-

a few worldly and humorous pieces. It abounds in approaches to
the ballad manner.

[18] See *Notes and Queries*, 1905. Christ is referred to again and
again as a "knight" in many religious songs from the *Love Rune*
of Thomas de Hales onward.

pear, a closer connection in lyrical quality and in the use
of refrains and repetition is afforded by the religious lyrics.
The closest approaches which one finds to the ballad man-
ner are the religious pieces like those in the Sloane and the
Hill manuscripts.

Lyrical narratives in couplet and quatrain form are ad-
mitted as ballads.   If the three-line carol stave — which
dropped from use because a less suitable form for narra-
tive verse [19]— were recognized also, such pieces as the fol-
lowing narrative carol [20] might be termed ballads.   Both
the couplet and the carol stave had wide lyrical popularity
earlier than the quatrain.

> Owt of the est a sterre shon bright
> For to shew thre kingis light,
> Which had ferre traveled day & nyght
>   To seke that lord that all hath sent.
>
> Therof hard kyng Herode anon,
> That III kingis shuld cum thorow his regyon,
> To seke a child that pere had non,
>   And after them sone he sent.
>
> Kyng Herode cried to them on hye:
> "Ye go to seke a child truly;
> Go forth & cum agayn me by,
>   & tell me wher that he is lent."
>
> Forth they went by the sterres leme,
> Till they com to mery Bethlehem;
> Ther they fond that swet barn-teme
>   That sith for vs his blode hath spent.

[19] The iteration of triple rhyme brings monotony and checks the
speed of the narrative.   Just as with the ballad, so with the popular
hymn stanza, the three-line form was replaced by the quatrain.

[20] MS. Balliol 354.   *Richard Hill's Commonplace Book.*   Ed. Dy-
boski, E. E. T. S., Extra Series, 101 (1907), p. 1.

Balthasar kneled first a down
& said: " Hayll, Kyng, most of renown,
And of all kyngis thou berist the crown,
  Therfor with gold I the present."

Melchior kneled down in that stede
& said: " Hayll, Lord, in thy pryest-hede.
Receyve ensence to thy manhede,
  I brynge it with a good entent."

Jasper kneled down in that stede
& said: " Hayll, Lord, in thy knyghthede,
I offer the myrre to thy godhede,
  For thou art he that all hath sent."

Now lordis & ladys in riche aray,
Lyfte vp your hartis vpon this day,
& ever to God lett vs pray,
  That on the rode was rent.

The following from the Hill manuscript [21] is not in-
cluded or mentioned by Professor Child, yet, if instead of
being narrated in the first person like a few of the ballads
it were narrated in the third, like most of them, and if it
were in couplet or in the more usual quatrain form instead
of in monorhyme quatrains, who would hesitate to classify
it as a ballad?   It is clearly akin to the *Judas* which is so
classified.

" O my harte is wo! "   Mary she sayd so,
" For to se my dere son dye; & sonnes haue I no mo."

" Whan that my swete son was xxxti wynter old,
Than the traytor Judas wexed very bold;
For xxxti platis of money, his master he had sold;

[21] Ed. Dyboski, E. E. T. S., 101, p. 40.

But whan I it wyst, lord my hart was cold.
 O, my hart is wo!" [Mary, she sayd so,
 " For to se my dere son dye; & sonnes haue I no mo."]

" Vpon Shere Thursday than truly it was,
On my sonnes deth that Judas did on passe;
Many were the fals Jewes that folowed hym by trace,
& there, beffore them all, he kyssed my sonnes face.
 O, my hart [is wo!" Mary, she sayd so,
 " For to se my dere son dye; & sonnes haue I no mo."]

" My son, beffore Pilat browght was he;
& Peter said III tymes he knew hym not perde.
Pylat said vnto the Jewes: ' What say ye?'
Than they cryed with on voys: ' Crucyfyge!'
 O, my hart is woo!" [Mary, she sayd so,
 " For to se my dere son dye; & sonnes haue I no mo."]

" On Good Friday at the mownt of Caluary
My son was don on the crosse, naled with nalis III,
Of all the frendis that he had, neuer on could he see,
But jentyll the evangelist, that still stode hym by.
 O, my hart [is wo!" Mary, she sayd so,
 " For to se my dere son dye; & sonnes haue I no mo."]

" Thowgh I were sorowful, no man haue at yt wonder;
for howge was the erth-quak, horyble was the thonder;
I loked on my swet son on the cross that stod vnder;
Then cam Lungeus with a spere & clift his hart in sonder.
 O, my [hart is wo!" Mary, she sayd so,
 " For to se my dere son dye; & sonnes haue I no mo."]

Its relation to the *Judas* is seen when the two are read
side by side. The latter opens: —

Hit wes upon a Scerethorsday that vre louerd aros;
Ful milde were the wordes he spec to Iudas.

> " Iudas, thou most to Iurselem, oure mete for to bugge;
> Thritti platen of seluer thou bere up othi ruggi. . . ."

It is a somewhat arbitrary distinction which admits the
second piece as a ballad and denies to the more lyrical one
such classification. The pieces might well have emerged
from the same types of authorship and audience. The
thirteenth-century ballad of *The Twelfth Day* in the
same Trinity College manuscript and in the same hand-
writing as the *Judas,* but in more elaborate stanza form,
has already been mentioned. It opens: —

> Wolle ye iheren of twelte day, wou the present was ibroust.
> In to betlem ther iesus lay, ther thre kinges him habbet isoust.
> a sterre wiset hem the wey, suc has neuer non iwroust,
> ne werede he nouther fou ne grey, the louerd that us alle hauet
>   iwroust.

It seems difficult to believe that such religious pieces as
the *Judas* and the *St. Stephen and Herod* represent a type
to be developed by the addition of narrative from the *secu-
lar* carol or dance song, as suggested by Professor Ker.[22]
They owe much to religious songs. Perhaps if we note that
refrains of both types, of secular dance songs and of
religious songs, precede the appearance of refrains in the
English and Scottish ballads (these appear mostly in the
late sixteenth and the seventeenth centuries); if we rec-
ognize as most essential in the ballads a narrative element
to be presented in the manner of the religious pieces; and
if we impose the somewhat arbitrary condition of couplet
or quatrain form, barring the three-line carol stave, qua-
train monorhyme, and related forms, we are on fairly safe
ground. Certainly it seems quite unnecessary to retain

22 *English Literature: Mediæval* (1912). Home University Lib-
rary edition, p. 159.

the hypothesis of connection with dance-song origin,
whether aristocratic, like the secular carols of Chaucer's
time, or of the folk. Behind the earliest ballad texts
which remain to us one finds no traces of affiliation with
secular dance songs.

The handling of the refrain is striking in the following
piece, also from the Hill manuscript, which, except for its
brevity and for our traditional rejection of narratives in
carol-stave form, we should classify as a ballad.[23]

THE STONING OF ST. STEPHEN

Whan seynt Stevyn was at Jeruzalem,
Godis lawes he loved to lerne;
That made the Jewes to cry so clere & clen,
 Lapidaverunt Stephanum,
  Nowe syng we both all & sum:
  Lapidauerunt Stephanum.

The Jewes that were both false & fell,
Against seynt Stephyn they were cruell,
Hym to sle they made gret yell,
 & lapidaverunt Stephanum
  Nowe syng we, etc.

They pullid hym with-owt the town,
& than he mekely kneled down,
While the Jewes crakkyd his crown,
 Quia lapidaverunt Stephanum,
  Nowe syng we, etc.

Gret stones & bones at hym they caste,
Veynes & bones of hym they braste,
& they kylled hym at the laste,

[23] E. E. T. S., 101 (1907), p. 32. *The Stoning of St. Stephen* is
not mentioned by Professor Child. Both the St. Stephen pieces are
probably to be classed as St. Stephen day songs or carols.

Quia lapidauerunt Stephanum.
  Nowe syng we, etc.

Pray we all that now be here,
Vnto seynt Stephyn, that marter clere,
To save vs all from the fendis fere.
  Lapidauerunt Stephanum.
    Nowe syng we, etc.

It arrays itself alongside *St. Stephen and Herod.* The
two lyrics, one adjudged to be a ballad, the other not to be
one, are at least not so different in type as to make neces-
sary the hypothesis of an utterly different mode of origin
for the second. *The Stoning of St. Stephen* is the more
lyrical of the two narratives and, unlike the earlier piece,
it is provided with a refrain.

The following affords yet another illustration of eccle-
siastical, or semi-ecclesiastical, narrative song, from the
period when Child ballads were not yet abundant.[24]

The Murder of Thomas a Beket

Lystyn, lordyngis both gret & small,
I will you tell a wonder tale,
Howe holy chirch was browght in bale
  Cum magna iniuria.
    A, a, a, a! nunc gaudet ecclesia.

The gretteste clark in this londe,
Thomas of Canturbury, I vnderstonde,
Slayn he was with wykyd honde,
  Malorum potencia.
    A, a, a, a! nunc gaudet ecclesia.

[24] Balliol MS. 354 E. E. T. S., 101, p. 31.   The triple rhyme stanza
of these ecclesiastical ballads appears also in Miracle plays, e. g.,
the Chester *Noah's Flood.*

The knyghtis were sent from Harry the kynge,
That day they dide a wykid thynge,
Wykyd men, with-owt lesynge,
   Per regis imperia.
     A, a, a, a! nunc gaudet ecclesia.

They sowght the bisshop all a-bowt,
With-in his place, and with-out,
Of Jhesu Crist they had no dowght
   Per sua malicia.
     A, a, a, a! nunc gaudet ecclesia.

They opened ther mowthes wonderly wide,
& spake to hym with myche pryde:
" Traytor, here thow shalt abide,
   Ferens mortis tedia."
     A, a, a, a! nunc gaudet ecclesia.

Beffore the auter he kneled down,
& than they pared his crown,
& stered his braynes vp so down,
   Optans celi gawdia.
     A, a, a, a! nunc gaudet ecclesia.

Recognition of song-narratives in carol stave, as well as of those in couplet and quatrain form, would admit this piece also among ballads.

III — BALLADS AND CLERICALS

Clericals are known to have composed and sung religious lyrics; but an alternative hypothesis from that of direct ecclesiastical creation is that a lyric type successfully developed by minstrels, namely the song-story — existing alongside the songs of eulogy, of derision, the love songs, and other matter which they had in stock for entertainment — was adopted and made use of for its own

ends by the church.   There would be abundant parallels
for such a taking over.   Ritson [25] speaks of the utilization
of popular airs by the Methodists of his day, much as they
had been utilized earlier by the Puritans.   The practice
was not unknown to the evangelists Moody and Sankey and
is not extinct among revivalists of the present time.
Sumer is icumen in of the thirteenth century perhaps owes
its preservation to the religious words written below the
secular ones in the manuscript which has come down to us,
and there are other examples in old manuscripts of relig-
ious adaptation of secular lyrics.   To find illustration
farther back, Ealdhelm is described by William of Malmes-
bury [26] as sometimes standing in gleeman's garb on a
bridge and inserting words of scriptural content into his
lighter songs — an early example of the connection be-
tween the church and songs for the common folk.   After
the Conquest, with the coming of a new type of song, the
employment of the short recited tale or of the sung story
for popularizing religious material might well have pro-
duced pieces like the thirteenth-century *Judas* or the later
St. Stephen and Herod or *Inter Diabolus et Virgo*.   If the
modes of the church were often utilized for secular poetry,
the contrary tendency, the adoption of what was popular
by the church, is also marked.   The great days of the min-
strels were the eleventh, twelfth, and thirteenth centuries,
and the days of their break-up the fifteenth and the six-
teenth centuries.   Warton thought that " some of our
greater monasteries kept minstrels of their own in regular

[25] *Dissertation on Ancient Songs and Music*, prefixed to *Ancient
Songs and Ballads*.   Vol. I (ed. of 1829), p. lxxviii.

[26] *De Gestis Pontificum Anglorum.   Chronicles and Memorials of
Great Britain and Ireland during the Middle Ages.*   Published under
the direction of the Master of the Rolls, 1858–99, p. 336.

pay." [27]   The class of minstrels indicated by Thomas de
Cabham, a thirteenth-century archbishop of Canterbury, as
to be tolerated while other classes deserved to be con-
demned, was the class which sang the deeds of princes and
the lives of saints.[28]   When minstrels had ecclesiastical
audiences, religious matter or national or heroic matter
might come from them appropriately.   A testimony re-
mains concerning the songs of a minstrel Herbert before
the prior of St. Swithin's when he entertained his bishop
at Winchester in the fourteenth century (1338), and they
were songs of Colbrand (Guy of Warwick) and of the de-
liverance by miracle of Queen Emma.[29]   From the fif-
teenth century is a record of a song of the early Christian
legend of the Seven Sleepers of Ephesus given at an Epiph-
any entertainment at Bicester in 1432.[30]   These may
not have been ballads, but they fall in the ballad period and
their material is of the type, the deeds of princes and the
lives of saints and martyrs, which was countenanced by de
Cabham.

A piece of first-hand evidence concerning the value of
the harper and his harp to a discriminating prelate is re-

[27] There are many records of payments to minstrels extant in
account books of Durham Priory, from the thirteenth century on-
ward, and from Maxtoke and Thetford Priories from the fifteenth
century. See. E. K. Chambers, *The Mediæval Stage.*

[28] *Penitential,* printed by B. Hauréau, *Notices et Extraits de
Manuscrits,* xxiv, ii, 284, from *Bib. Nat. Lat.* 3218 and 3529. Sunt
autem alii, qui dicuntur ioculatores, qui cantant gesta principum et
vitam sanctorum, et faciunt solatia hominibus vel in aegritudinibus
suis vel in angustiis . . . et non faciunt etc. . . . Si autem non
faciunt talia, sed cantant in instrumentis suis gesta principum et
alia talia utilia ut faciant solatia hominibus, sicut supradictum est,
bene possunt sustineri tales, sicut ait Alexander papa.

[29] See Warton, *History of English Poetry,* ed. of 1840, pp. 81, 82.
[30] Kennet, *Parochial Antiquities* (1695), ed. of 1818.

lated by Robert Manning of Brunne in an account of Robert Grosseteste, Bishop of Lincoln, who died in 1253. Bishop Grosseteste wrote in English as well as Latin, translating the allegorical *Castel of Love* into English for the sake of the ignorant.   He recognized that the common people had to be reached in their own tongue.   Robert Manning's testimony is as follows: [31]

> Y shall yow telle, as y haue herd
> Of the bysshope Seynt Roberd;
> Hys toname ys Grostest
> Of Lynkolne, so seyth the gest.
> He loued moche to here the harpe,
> For mannys wytte hyt makyth sharpe;
> Next hys chaumbre, beside hys stody,
> Hys harpers chaumbre was fast thereby.
> Many tymes, be nyhtys and dayys,
> He had solace of notes and layys.
> One asked hym onys, resun why
> He hadde delyte yn mynstralsy:
> He answerede hym on thys manere,
> Why he helde the harper so dere,
> The vertu of the harpe, thurgh skylle & ryght
> Wyl destroye the fendes myght,
> And to the croys by gode skylle
> Ys the harpe lykened weyle. . . .
> The harpe therof me ofte mones;
> Of the ioye and of the blys
> Where God hymself wonys and ys.
> Thare-fore, gode men, ye shul lere,
> Whan ye any glemen here,
> To wurschep God at youre powere,
> As Dauyd seyth yn the sautere,
> Yn harpe, yn thabour, and symphan gle,
> Wurschepe God, yn troumpes and sautre,

---

[31] *Handlyng Synne*, ed. F. J. Furnivall, E. E. T. S., 119.

Yn cordes, an organes, and bellys ryngyng,
Yn al these, wurschepe ye heuene kyng.
Yf ye do thus, y sey hardly,
Ye mow here youre mynstralsy.

The alternative possibilities (granting that religious ballads are an early type) are: that short narrative lyrics on ecclesiastical themes emerged directly from clericals and that the type was later secularized; or that they emerged from the minstrels, and ecclesiastics availed themselves of the type; or that minstrels were solely responsible for the early religious ballads, composing them for audiences for whom they were especially suitable. But when lingering over these hypotheses, one is inclined to give the church a greater share of responsibility for the earliest ballads than the third hypothesis assumes.

If the earliest mediæval ballads, meaning by ballads lyrical stories of the type collected by Professor Child, were contemporaneously on both religious and heroic subjects, it is chance, or else the interest of ecclesiastics, that has preserved for us specimens of the one type and not of the other. If the heroic type, chronicle or legendary, was as early as the religious, early examples have not remained to show it. Against the hypothesis of contemporaneousness is the circumstance that songs of all other kinds, minstrel and popular, satires, eulogies of princes and heroes, songs of victories, love songs, songs of disparagement or derision, humorous songs, drinking songs, and the like, have descended to us from the Middle Ages. If ballads of the heroic type existed early, they should have appeared at least as early as the thirteenth century. The wish to impress sacred story may well have afforded the impulse to present such narratives in a short lyrical way, and the presence of narrative is the fundamental *differentia,* the quality distinguishing it from other folk-song, of the ballad as a lyric type.

A refrain is not present in the earliest ballad texts nor in the fifteenth-century ballads,[32] including the Robin Hood pieces. Refrains do not appear in ballads until the sixteenth century, though they are frequent in early lyrics of other types. Moreover, they are sufficiently accounted for in the proportion of ballads in which they are present (not more than a fourth) by the fact that the ballads were sung. Hymns and carols and many love songs have refrains, and the ballad refrains were handled on the whole in their way. They do not resemble the fundamental iterative lines of dance songs, around which the latter songs as a class are built.[33] Ballad refrains are added from the outside and are not stable even for the same text, while the refrain is the most identifying feature of the average traditional dance song. It is well established that the earliest mediæval dance songs were not ballads; though the latter came to be used occasionally as dance songs, consistently as such in Denmark. The fundamental characteristic of ballads, the point of departure for their differentiation as a lyric type, would be their presentation of characters and story in a lyrical way, suitable for short recital or for song. It would not be the presence of a refrain, nor of incremental repetition, nor parallelism of line structure; for both are often absent from ballads and often present in other types of folk-song. A "situation" mode

[32] Unless in *Robin and Gandeleyn.* If a refrain is present in this ballad it is extraneous to the stanza structure, not part of it. The stanzas of the ballad so vary in form and length as to make them seem more suitable for recital than for singing.

[33] See Chapter II.

of narration is not perhaps fundamental, but such a mode would be natural in a lyric to be recited dramatically like the *Judas* perhaps, or like *St. Stephen and Herod;* or it might be developed, like repetition and parallelism, in traditional preservation.   Ballad creation has for its motivating impulse the circumstance that characters and their story are to be brought before hearers, not in a narrative to be read, but briefly and memorably and dramatically in a recitational or song way.   Only stories which lend themselves well to such handling are eligible material.

It is possible that very widespread diffusion for the ballads, especially for the secular ballads, their composition in quantity and their popular currency, may have come later than is generally assumed.   They cannot have been very abundant when the makers of the Sloane MS. 2593 and the Balliol MS. 354 made their collections.   These men obviously had a taste for popular verse, yet compared to their display of related types of folk-verse, of approaches to ballads, their showing of ballads proper is meager. Had many ballads of the Child type been in general circulation in Southern England before the Elizabethan period, had this type of verse been so recognized, so distinctive and current as it was in the later sixteenth and the seventeenth centuries, the makers of these, like the makers of later manuscript books, might have been expected to give proportionate space to ballads in their pages.

The number of early religious ballads remaining is somewhat slender, too slender for a very solid structure to be based upon them; but their evidence is the most authentic that we have.   The subject of ballad origins may well be re-examined from the angle of approach which these, our earliest ballad texts, suggest.   The species next to fix attention upon itself is the outlaw ballad of the fifteenth and early sixteenth centuries; but the outlaw ballads come too late for dependable significance. Some were plainly to be recited; [34] in general they lack the refrain element; and they afford no help in explaining the origin of the lyrical species. The suggestion which relates the early ballads to the religious, not the secular, carols as a type of folk-song, which assumes ecclesiastical emergence for the ballads prior to their minstrel popularity, or else early adoption by ecclesiastics of a new minstrel lyric type, has the distinction of novelty, whether or not it seem likely. And it is based on fact, not conjecture. The possibility that ballad literature began with clericals deserves to be taken into account, alongside the hypotheses of ballad origin which have been brought forward in the past.

Few having knowledge of the shifting types and styles of popular song would maintain that the folk-songs, the dance songs, if you will, of the Anglo-Saxons before the Norman Conquest were of the structure and type of the Child ballads. The patterns which these exhibit arose later. Nor were the old heroic lyrics of the Germanic peoples, whether narrative or not, of the type of the Child ballads. In the hypothesis that mediæval ballad literature emerged under the influence of clericals, or in something like it, may perhaps be found the explanation best satisfying all the conditions. Examination is desirable, from this angle of approach, of the early lyrical verse of other leading European peoples. The ballad documents of Con-

[34] See the testimony concerning " robene hude and litil ihone " and the tale of the " zong tamlene " listed in *The Complaynt of Scotland*, 1549. Edited by J. A. H. Murray, E. E. T. S. (1872). vol. I, p. 63.

tinental literatures are no earlier than the English, if so early; but the more the available evidence, the better for the investigator. A scrutiny of them might lend support to the suggestions brought forward here, or it might contradict them, or it might bring light from some unexpected source.

CHAPTER VI

BALLADRY IN AMERICA

American interest in ballads and in other folk-songs has arisen mainly as an aftermath of the quest of Old World traditional texts on this side of the Atlantic. Some impulse has come from other sources. The collection and preservation of many popular songs and ballads of the Revolution and of the Civil War is to be credited to historians, although no consistent effort was made at the psychological time to assemble and to preserve such pieces. Of leading importance was the impetus given to the recovery of American folk-song by Professor Francis James Child. He accumulated a vast number of broadsides and orally preserved texts in the Harvard University library, and since his death material has been added steadily through the vigilant personal interest and the stimulus to others of Professor G. L. Kittredge. Professor Kittredge has encouraged the gathering and identification of traditional texts from various parts of the United States for many years, and students of folk-song are deeply in his debt. Another historic name among scholars is that of W. W. Newell, a pioneer collector of the songs and games of American children and a founder of the American Folk-Lore Society. In recent decades, many regional collectors have gathered material, especially along the Atlantic coast, in the South, and in the Central West, and the realization has arisen that there is a picturesque body of orally preserved song on this side of the Atlantic. Such traditional material is of interest to the lover of poetry for the occasional flashes of quality which it exhibits and for its contrast to book poetry. It is of interest to the student of literature for the value as social documents of the pieces it preserves, and for the evidence which they give concerning the development and transmission of folk-songs. Enough material is already available to throw light on many points of geographical distribution, and of song history, and to establish some main lines of grouping.

I — OLD-WORLD BALLADS AND SONGS IN AMERICA

Of the types of folk-song existent in America, the legendary and romantic ballads of England and Scotland, large numbers of which have emigrated to the New World, are those which have been recovered and examined with the greatest interest. They have found many enthusiastic collectors.[1] If they have not quite monopolized the fore-

---

[1] Some leading collectors are: H. G. Shearin and J. H. Coombs for the Cumberland mountains, *Syllabus of Kentucky Folk-Song* (1911); C. Alphonso Smith for Virginia (see *infra*, note 2); Reed Smith for South Carolina (see *infra*, note 2); H. M. Belden for Missouri, *Journal of American Folk-Lore*, vols. 19, 20, 23; A. H. Tolman for Illinois, *ibid.*, vol. 29; Phillips Barry for New England, see many papers and texts in the *Journal of American Folk-Lore*, vol. 14 and following; Cecil Sharp and Olive Dame Campbell, *Folk-Song of the Southern Appalachians* (1917); Josephine McGill, *Folk-Song of the Kentucky Mountains* (1917); E. F. Piper for Iowa (unpublished); Louise Pound, *Folk-Song of Nebraska and the Central West: A Syllabus* (1915). By far the largest and most important collection is in the Harvard library.

Illustrative American traditional songs are accessible in the present writer's *Oral Verse in the United States*, 1921.

The discussion of balladry in America in the present chapter is

ground in discussions of American folk-song they have nearly done so. They constitute the folk-pieces most archaic in style and having the longest history. They are those most easily sought and identified by the average searcher for traditional material, since they are to be found in printed collections, and there is no little mystery concerning their origin. They have reached this country in various ways. Some surely were brought over by the early colonists and were handed down by their descendants. Others may have been brought over not long after by sailors or returned travellers. Still others enter from time to time with newcomers from the British Isles. The process of importation has not quite ceased.

Old World ballads in the United States are, on the whole, best recovered from regions where the songs and song modes of the past have not been displaced by the entrance of later songs and song modes. At times such texts come to light in cities, but much more characteristically they are salvaged from remote and isolated communities unsupplied with later popular songs and relying still upon the entertainment of song, instead of upon the variety of present devices available for passing the time of young and old. Outlying rural districts, particularly mountain communities, yield especial results. The best hunting grounds for collectors have been the North Atlantic States and the Southern mountains, like the Cumberland mountains — the Appalachian region in general; that is, those regions of the United States which were earliest

indebted in scattered passages to the author's discussion of oral literature in the United States in the *Cambridge History of American Literature*, vol. III. Occasionally it uses the same material in illustration.

settled.   In the West, villages and isolated farms and
ranches yield an occasional Old World ballad, but a text
is likely to be recovered wherever some newcomer from
an older community has settled, or, especially, some
immigrant to the New World; or where the descendants
of such newcomers have good memories for their parents'
songs.   A few traditional ballads have lingered as nursery
songs; for example *Lord Randal, The Two Brothers,* and
Lamkin.

Texts or fragments of nearly 80 of the 305 ballads in-
cluded in the Child collection have been recovered in the
United States,[2] mainly from oral sources, sometimes from
manuscript books.   As regards distribution, the Southern
mountains and the New England states have yielded the
greatest returns, though some texts have been recovered
from the central West and even from the far West.   Lead-
ing in popularity among them is *Barbara Allen's Cru-
elty:* —[3]

> 'Twas in the merry month of May
> When the green buds were a-swelling
> Sweet William on his death bed lay
> For the love of Barbara Allen.

Another widely current favorite is *Lord Lovel,* sometimes
transformed to *Lord Lover,* whose hero goes on a journey
after bidding farewell to his sweetheart, returns, and finds
her dead.

[2] See especially Reed Smith, *The Traditional Ballad in the South,
Journal of American Folk-Lore,* vol. 27, pp. 55–66; *ibid.,* 28, pp. 199–
203.   C. Alphonso Smith *Ballads Surviving in the United States,
The Musical Quarterly,* vol. II, pp. 109–129.

[3] Unless indicated otherwise, the texts of Old World songs quoted
in the following pages are central Western.

> " O where are you going, Lord Lovel ? " she said,
> " O where are you going ? " says she.
> " I'm going, my lady Nancy Bell,
> Strange countries for to see, see, see,
> Strange countries for to see."

Another popular importation is the ballad of *Lord Bate-man* (Bakeman, Bayham, etc.), the Young Beichan of the Scottish ballad, who is rescued from a Turkish prison by his captor's daughter. She follows him seven years later to his own country, arrives on the eve of his wedding to another, and herself becomes his bride. *The Two Sisters,* one of whom pushes the other into a mill stream where she is drowned, and *Geordie,* also have considerable currency. *Lord Randal* roams the country under many aliases. As recovered in a Colorado railway camp [4] the song tells the tragic story of Johnny Randall.

> " Where was you last night, Johnny Randall, my son?
> Where was you last night, my heart's loving one ? "
> " A-fishing, a-fowling, mother make my bed soon,
> For I'm sick at my heart and I fain would lie down."

He becomes Jimmy Randall in Illinois, Jimmy Ransing in Indiana, Johnny Ramble in Ohio, and Johnny Ran-dolph in North Carolina. Most of the Old World ballads preserved in the United States are upon themes of romantic love, of tragedy, and adventure. *Little Harry Hughes,* deriving from *Sir Hugh and the Jew's Daughter,* is a legacy of the mediæval superstitions against the Jews. A riddle ballad remains, *The Cambric Shirt,* which bears some relation to *The Elfin Knight,* and a few sea pieces survive, like *The Three Sailor Boys,* related to *The Mer-*

[4] By H. C. House. See *Modern Language Notes,* vol. 17, p. 6.

maid, and *The Golden Vanity,* or *The Lowlands Low.*
What has happened to these Old World pieces in the
New? Have they improved or decayed from their Eng-
lish and Scottish originals? Some are spun out by repe-
tition and iteration and lose their cohesion in garrulous-
ness. Most are made over to agree with a democratic en-
vironment and with the horizons of their singers. The
Child ballads have to do with the high born. They tell
of the adventures of kings and princesses and nobles, com-
bats, the chase, clan feuds, the domestic tragedies of
aristocrats. These pass in America into plebeian narra-
tives of homelier setting; the unknown, in names, or ob-
jects, or descriptive terms, is made over into the known, in
the folk-etymological manner. Localizations are changed,
as well as names and characters. Serious events are often
vulgarized or made commonplace. The romantic aristo-
cratic elements are dimmed. Lord Randal's metamor-
phosis has been mentioned. In many American versions,
Sir John and Sir Hugh of *The Two Brothers* become two
little schoolboys. Sometimes the supernatural is lost, as
when the devil in some versions of *The Ship's Carpenter*
becomes a returned lover; or when, as in some versions of
The Farmer's Curst Wife, he disappears. A few have
been utilized as game or dance songs, as *Barbara Allen's
Cruelty* and *The Two Sisters.* *The Two Brothers* in its
Nebraska version, seems to be turning into a Western
song: —

> "O what shall I tell your true love, John,
>   If she inquires for you?"
> "O tell her I'm dead and lying in my grave,
>   Way out in Idaho."

Each ballad may be accommodated to a variety of melodies; it is a safe generalization that the texts of ballads are more constant than the melodies. Occasionally ballads cross or become disordered and a new amalgam song emerges.[5] Rarely mannerisms of the English and Scottish ballads spread to indigenous pieces. On the whole, the degenerative effects of oral preservation are well exemplified by the mass of Old World pieces which have been recovered in America. Not brought over, or dying out early if they were brought over, are heroic tales and border ballads, and songs turning on local customs, as harvest songs, carols, and the like.

But the legendary English and Scottish ballads reaching America are not the only ballads to be imported. In later British balladry commonplace characters replace the aristocrats and other styles the minstrel style. British ballads of this later type, on the themes of the broadside press of the last two centuries, have far greater currency in the United States than do the legendary and romantic ballads. Of this type is *The Butcher's Boy,* in one text of which a girl from Jersey City loves a butcher's boy, but he deserts her for another " because she has more gold than I." At the close of the song the girl hangs herself, leaving lines pinned on her breast. It is related to the British *A Brisk Young Lover. The Boston Burglar,* or *Charleston,* is related to *A Sheffield Apprentice.* The speaker says that he was brought up by honest parents but his " character was taken " and he could not be cleared. He was sent as the " Boston Burglar " to Charleston.

---

[5] See H. M. Belden, *Folk Song in America — Some Recent Publications. Modern Language Notes,* vol. 34, p. 139.

> And every station I would pass
> I'd hear the people say,
> There goes a Boston burgular,
> See he's all bound in iron.

Jack Williams is a boatman by trade. For the sake of a girl he took to robbing and was brought back to Sing Sing (Newgate): —

> On Bowery (Chatton) street I did reside,
> Where the people did me know,
> I fell in love with a pretty girl,
> She proved my overthrow.

Of greater interest is *Betsy Brown,* which derives obviously from colonial days.[6] A woman's son, Johnny, loves Betsy the servant. The mother takes Betsy to the seaside where she sells her across to "verginny." Her son dies and the mother repents her act too late. This ballad has been recovered from New England, the central West, and the far West. A Nebraska text is in manuscript form and preserves the story pretty completely.

> O son, O son, your love's in vain for we sold betsy cross the
>   main;
> My son, my son, my son, says she, your bringing scandal on
>   you and me,
> I would rather see your corpse lie dead than to marry betsy a
>   servant maid.

Older still, in all probability, is *The Death of a Romish Lady* which has also reached the central West. It tells the story of a lady who became a convert to Protestantism, possessed a Bible, and would not " bow to idols." For

5 C. H. Firth prints a text in *An American Garland* (1915), p. 69.

this her cruel mother had her brought before priests and burned.

> There lived a Romish lady
> Brought up in proper array,
> Her mother oftimes told her
> She must the priest obey.

This is to be identified with the Elizabethan " It was a lady's daughter, of Paris properly," introduced into Fletcher's *Knight of the Burning Pestle*. The earliest text preserved is a reprint from the times of Charles II.[7] The American texts have been shortened a little, in three centuries, and show simplification, but the original narrative is well preserved.

Of Old World provenance is also the widely diffused *Willie and Mary* or the *Bedroom Window*, sometimes known also as *The Drowsy Sleeper*. It hints a tragedy not carried out in most texts.

> " O Mary dear, go ask your father
> If you my wedded bride can be.
> If he says nay then come and tell me,
> And I no more will trouble thee."

> " O Willie dear, I dare not ask him,
> For he lies on his bed of rest,
> And by his side there lies a dagger
> To pierce the one that I love best."

Songs of the pirate Captain Kidd and of Turpin the highwayman still have currency in American folk-song. *Father Grumble*, or *Old Grumble*, has many aliases and is a song of Old World pedigree, but the same story is

[7] Accessible in *The Roxburgh Ballads*, vol. I, p. 43.

always told. Father and Mother Grumble exchange tasks
for the day and the former comes to grief.

> Father Grumble he did say,
> As sure as the moss round a tree,
> That he could do more work in a day
> Than his wife could do in three, three,
> That he could do more work in a day
> Than his wife could do in three.

Other importations are *The Farmer's Boy*, the story of a
poor boy who comes to a farmer's door, and in the course
of time marries the farmer's daughter and inherits the
land, *The Soldier*, who when eloping with a lady with
a fortune is met by the father and armed men, *The Banks
of Claudy* or *The Lover's Return*, *The Prentice Boy* or
Cupid's Garden, *The Rich Merchant of London* whose
daughter drinks poison because loving against her father's
wishes, the tragedies of *Lady Caroline of Edinboro Town*,
and of *Mary of the Wild Moor* or *The Village Bride*,
and the familiar songs, *Babes in the Woods*, *Billy Boy*,
and *The Courtship of the Frog and the Mouse*.

The foregoing pieces will serve to illustrate the im-
ported material, its diffusion, persistence, and the types of
plots and the patterns of song which have lingered in the
popular consciousness. Among Old World importations,
it is the sensational story song, and the humorous ballad
or song, which have shown the greatest vitality.

II — INDIGENOUS BALLADS AND SONGS

Alongside importations from the Old World, many
types of indigenous song have developed in America.
There are picturesque songs of pioneer and Western life,

songs of criminals and outlaws, of soldiers and wars, of tragedies and disasters, songs of the tragic death of a girl, dying messages and confessions, and songs of the lost at sea. Sentimental songs play an important rôle, and religious and moralizing songs, political campaign songs, humorous songs, and negro or pseudo-negro and Indian songs appear. Some of these are sufficiently narrative to deserve classification as ballads, and all should have interest for collectors. Generalizations concerning folk-song are thrown out of focus and are undependable when but one type of piece is sought out and studied. All types of songs are folk-songs, for the literary historian, which fulfill two tests. The people must like them and sing them — they must have " lived in the folk-mouth " — and they must have persisted in oral currency through a fair period of years. They must have achieved an existence not dependent upon a printed original. Questions of origin, quality, technique, or style, are secondary. Attempts at differentiating traditional songs into *popular songs* or songs made " for " the people, and *folk-songs* or songs made " by " the people, based on some hypothetical manner of origin or on the continuation of a mediæval style, have been demonstrated many times, when applied to some body of folk-song, to be undependable and unsafe. Whatever has commended itself to the folk-consciousness and has established currency for itself apart from written sources is genuine folk-literature.

Before the American Revolution, most folk-song was probably imported, either orally or in broadside versions; but there were also historical pieces that were indigenous. Some early ballads popular in New England, the texts of which have not been preserved are: *The Gallant*

Church, Smith's Affair at Sidelong Hill, and *The God-less French Soldier.*[8] *Lovewell's Fight* is the oldest re-maining historical ballad composed in America of which texts are available. It records a contest with the Indians in Maine, May 8, 1725. A text put into print about a hundred years later begins —

> What time the noble Lovewell came
>   With fifty men from Dunstable
> The cruel Pequatt tribe to tame
>   With arms and bloodshed terrible —

This theme was treated by Longfellow in his early poem, *The Battle of Lovell's Pond.*

Most of the songs and ballads of the Revolution, as brought together by collectors [9] from newspapers, period-icals, and broadsides, and from the memory of surviving soldiers, are semi-literary in character, composed to be sung to some familiar tune of English importation. The favorite ballad of the Revolution with literary historians is *Nathan Hale.* Many surviving pieces are travesties, many express the dissatisfaction of the colonists, and some derive from older pieces, as Major André's *The Cow Chace* which is based on the familiar ballad, *The Chevy Chase.* Most of the ballads remaining from this period are satirical.

A few indigenous pieces may derive from the War of 1812, such as *James Bird,* a ballad of a hero shot for desertion, a camp song in ridicule of General Packing-ham, and some verses beginning —

[8] See Professor M. C. Tyler, *History of American Colonial Liter-ature,* 1878.

[9] Chief among them is Frank Moore, *Songs and Ballads of the American Revolution,* 1856.

Then you sent out your Boxer to beat us all about;
We had an enterprising brig to beat the Boxer out.-. . .
Then towed her up to Portland and moved her off the town
To show the Sons of Liberty the Boxer of renown. . . .

and some stanzas which are still sung by children as a
marching song —

> We're marching down to old Quebec
> While the drums are loudly beating;
> The American boys have gained the day
> And the British are retreating.

The Texas Rangers, widely current throughout the
South and West, one text of which opens —

Come all you Texas Rangers wherever you may be,
I'll tell you of some trouble which happened unto me. . . .

sounds like an echo of the fight with the Mexicans at the
Alamo in 1833. It is modeled on and sung to the air
of the British *Nancy of Yarmouth.*

Songs remaining from the Civil War are often sen-
timental in character, like *When this Cruel War is Over,*
and *The Blue and the Gray,* which are of traceable origin
yet have entered widely into oral tradition. They are
songs not ballads. There were numerous camp songs on
sieges or battles but these faded early. Best remembered
in folk-song from the period of the Civil War are the
pseudo-negro songs, many of them the work of Stephen
C. Foster, Will S. Hays, or Henry C. Work, given dif-
fusion by the old-time itinerant minstrels. Songs of
this and related types from the period of the Civil War
are far more persistent than songs commemorating bat-
tles or political events. The popular *A Hot Time in the
Old Town Tonight,* modeled by its composer on a Creole

song and popularized during the Cuban War, does not
reflect directly the war that " floated " it, and the songs
universalized for England and America by the war of
1914–1918, *Tipperary, Keep the Home Fires Burning,
The Long, Long Trail, Pack Up Your Troubles in Your
Old Kit Bag, Over There,* do not commemorate its lead-
ing events. In the days of newspapers, ballads or songs
of battles or important political events are not in demand,
and do not come into existence.

Much larger than the rôle played by songs of historical
events or important movements is that played by senti-
mental romantic pieces or by adventure pieces, and by
certain widely diffused songs, mainly humorous, their
authorship and origin forgotten, which reflect emigrant
and frontier life, especially the rush for gold in 1849.
Such is *Joe Bowers,* once a freighter's favorite. The
song is supposed to be sung by a Missourian in California
about 1849–51, who had left behind his hometown sweet-
heart, Sally Black.[10]

> One day I got a letter,
>   'Twas from my brother Ike;
> It came from Old Missouri.
>   And all the way from Pike. . . .
> It said that Sal was false to me —
>   It made me cuss and swear —
> How she went and married a butcher,
>   And the butcher had red hair;
> And whether 'twas gal or boy
>   The letter never said,
> But that Sally had a baby,
>   And the baby's head was red.

[10] Unless indication otherwise is made, the text quoted is central
Western.

Here is to be grouped *Sweet Betsy from Pike,* a California immigrant song of the fifties, and that song of better quality, *The Days of Forty-Nine.*

> Since the days of old and the days of gold,
> And the days of Forty-Nine.

The Dreary Black Hills reflects the mining fever of one period in the West.

The Round House at Cheyenne is filled every night
With loafers and beggars of every kind of sight;
On their backs there's no clothes, boys, in their pockets no bills,
And they'll take off your scalp, boys, in those dreary Black Hills.

> Stay away, I say, stay away if you can,
> Far from that city they call Cheyenne;
> Where the blue waters roll and Comanche Bill
> Will take off your scalp in those dreary Black Hills.

Other sectional songs or humorous narratives or complaints are *Cheyenne Boys,* which has various aliases and changed locations, as *Mississippi Girls,* a narrative describing the ways of the "boys" and warning the girls not to marry them, *The Horse Wrangler,* who meets a cattle king and decides to try cow-punching, and *Starving to Death on a Government Claim* —

> Hurrah for Lane County, the land of the West,
> Where the farmers and laborers are ever at rest;
> There's nothing to do but to stick and remain,
> And starve like a dog on a government claim.

The three best known and most attractive pieces are all three adaptations, reflecting pioneer life. One is *O Bury*

Me not on the Lone Prairie, sometimes called *The Dying Cowboy,*[11]

> "O bury me not on the lone prairie."
> Those words came slow but mournfully
> From the pallid lips of a youth who lay
> On the cold damp ground at the close of day. . . .

Another is *The Cowboy's Lament,* also called sometimes *The Dying Cowboy* —

> As I walked through Tom Sherman's bar-room,
> Tom Sherman's bar-room on a bright summer's day,
> There I spied a handsome young cowboy,
> All dressed in white linen as though for the grave.

> Beat your drums lowly and play your fife slowly,
> Play the dead march as you bear me along,
> Take me to the graveyard and lay the sod o'er me,
> For I'm a young cowboy and I know I've done wrong.

This song exists in many variants, with changed names and localizations, and it has roamed pretty far from its eighteenth century original.[12]   The third is *My Little Old Sod Shanty* —

[11] Adapted from a sea song, the words of which were by W. H. Saunders, the music by G. N. Allen, beginning —

> "O bury me not in the deep, deep sea,"
> The words came low and mournfully, etc.

with the refrain

> "O bury me not in the deep deep sea,
> Where the billowy shroud will roll o'er me." . . .

[12] Mr. Phillips Barry has traced its history in *The Journal of American Folk-Lore,* vol. 24, pp. 341 ff.   It is from a song popular in Ireland in the eighteenth century, *The Unfortunate Rake.*   The refrain lines retain, somewhat incongruously, the suggestion of a military funeral appropriate enough in the original song.

> The hinges are of leather and the windows have no glass,
>> While the board roof lets the howling blizzard in,
> And I hear the hungry cayote as he slinks up through the grass,
>> Round the little old sod shanty on my claim.

The history of this song is sufficiently illustrative of the ways of folk-song to be worth recounting.[13] Like so many "Western" songs when their genealogy is followed out, it is not an indigenous Western piece but is an adaptation of an older song having great popularity, namely *The Little Old Log Cabin in the Lane* by Will S. Hays, a negro melody of the type familiarized by Stephen C. Foster's *My Old Kentucky Home,* or by *The Swanee River.*

> De hinges dey got rusted and de door has tumbled down,
>> An' de roof lets in de sunshine an' de rain,
> An' de only friend I've got now is dis good old dog of mine,
>> In de little old log cabin in de lane.

The Little Old Sod Shanty was printed somewhere about the later seventies or eighties in many Nebraska newspapers, with the statement that it could be sung to the tune of *The Little Old Log Cabin.* Some old settlers remember having cards with photographs of a sod shanty on one side and on the other the words of the song. The parody adapting the negro song to Western conditions was written probably by some one in this region.[14] Most versions of the song recovered by collectors come from Nebraska and the Dakotas, one from Texas. To continue the history of *The Little Old Log Cabin,* it is said that Ira

[13] See *The Pedigree of a Western Song, Modern Language Notes,* vol. 29, p. 30.

[14] According to his friends, by a Nebraskan named Emery Miller, when occupying a claim.

D. Sankey, the evangelist, adapted its well-known melody for C. W. Fry's religious lyric, *The Lily of the Valley,* or *I Have Found a Friend in Jesus.* In hymn number 105 of *Gospel Hymns No. 5,* widely used in the later decades of the nineteenth century, may be found the music which served for the various songs, the negro melody, and the " Western " and the religious songs.

There is little " romance " in most of these Western American pieces but they reflect the life of the Americans who sang and who sing them as faithfully as the English and Scottish traditional ballads reflect the life and ways of mediæval aristocrats. They are the most characteristically American of our folk-songs, and so wide is their diffusion that many are likely to survive for a generation or more. They exhibit the interests and tastes, the themes and song modes, of those among which they had currency.

Aside from these historical, frontier, and adventure pieces, there are now many short narrative pieces, orally preserved and apparently authorless, which may fairly be called indigenous ballads. And already they are marked in an instructive degree by fluctuation of text, variant versions, and local improvisations and additions. Most have a direct unsophisticated note and traces of rude power that lend them the appeal peculiar to folk song. An example of an indigenous ballad now current through the Middle West and as far Southwest as Texas is that of *Young Charlotte* who was frozen to death at her lover's side on her way to a ball.

Young Charlotte lived by a mountain side in a wild and lonely spot,
There was no village for miles around except her father's cot;

And yet on many a wintry night young boys would gather there —
Her father kept a social board, and she was very fair. . . .

"Such a dreadful night I never saw, my reins I can scarcely
hold,"
Young Charlottie then feebly said, "I am exceedingly cold,"
He cracked his whip and urged his speed much faster than
before,
While at least five other miles in silence had passed o'er.

Spoke Charles, "How fast the freezing ice is gathering on
my brow,"
Young Charlottie then feebly said, "I'm growing warmer
now." . . .

Investigation has shown that this ballad was the com-
position of a blind poet at Bensontown, Vermont, as far
back as 1835.[15] The good fortune of its attracting an
able investigator has cleared up for us its history. A
second New England product which has roamed every-
where is *Springfield Mountain,* the tragedy of a young
man mowing hay who was bitten by a "pizen serpent"
and died. Texts of this have been recovered from regions
as remote as Texas and Montana. Its historian was able
to trace its composition to the late eighteenth century.[16]
Of untraced origin but of still greater currency is *Poor
Lorella* (known also as *The Weeping Willow, Poor Flo-
ella, Flo Ella, Lurella, Lorla, Lorilla, The Jealous Lover,
Pearl Bryn,* etc.). Down in the valley, under the weep-
ing willow, lies Lorella in her "cold and silent grave."

15 See Phillips Barry, *The Journal of American Folk-Lore,* vol. 22,
pp. 365–73.

16 W. W. Newell, *Early American Ballads, The Journal of Ameri-
can Folk-Lore,* vol. 13, pp. 105–120. *Rattlesnake Song,* printed
among J. A. Lomax's *Cowboy Songs,* is obviously a somewhat
maudlin descendant of *Springfield Mountain.*

She died not from sickness or a broken heart, but was killed by her lover, who says that her parents will forgive him, since he expects to leave the country "never more for to return."

> Down on her knees before him
> She pleaded for her life,
> But deep into her bosom
> He plunged the fatal knife.

A similar piece, also untraced, is *The Old Shawnee*. A youth asks his sweetheart to take a walk, and talks of the day when their wedding is to be. She says she will never be his: —

> From my breast I drew a knife,
> And she gave a shrilling cry,
> "O Willie dear, don't murder me,
> For I am not prepared to die."

> Then I took her lily white hands
> And swung her around and again around,
> Until she fell in the waters cruel,
> And there I watched my true love drowned.

The Silver Dagger tells of a young man who courted a maiden, but his parents sought to part them on the ground of her poverty. When the girl learned this she wandered down by a river and stabbed herself with a silver dagger. Her lover heard her voice, rushed to her, found her dying, and killed himself with the same dagger.

To pass to illustration of American ballads of another type, *Jesse James* claims sympathy for its outlaw hero, an American Robin Hood. The ballad tells of his death through betrayal, killed by Robert Ford.

> Now Jesse had a wife to mourn for his life,
>   His children they were brave;
> 'Twas a dirty little coward that shot Mr. Howard
>   And laid poor Jesse in his grave.

This song is of late composition and has wide currency
but chance has failed to record its provenance. Texts
and the melody have been recovered by many collectors.
The Death of Garfield reflects moralizing delight in a
criminal's repentance, a stock motive in eighteenth and
nineteenth century popular song. Probably it is adapted
from an Old World piece.

> My sister came to prison to bid her last farewell,
> She threw her arms about me and wept most bitterly;
> She said, "My dearest brother, today you must die,
> For the murder of James A. Garfield upon the scafel high."

Fuller and Warren tells of a fatal quarrel between rival
lovers; *Casey Jones,* of the authorship of which there is
clearer record,[17] of a fatal railway run. Once well-
known ballads, now occasionally to be recovered from
oral tradition, are *The Wreck of the Lady Elgin,*[18] *The
Johnstown Flood,* and *The Burning of the Newhall House
at Milwaukee.* These may be termed ballads in that
they are simple lyrical narratives handed down orally,
though but for a short period, their authorship unknown
to their singers. The sensational stories they tell have
kept them alive for a while. Usually the tenure of life
of a ballad is longer when it tells some tragic personal
story.

---

[17] See *Railroad Men's Magazine*, May 1908, November 1910, Decem-
ber 1911, April 1912.
[18] By George F. Root.

As to modes of diffusion, these are many and varied, so far as can be determined by the collector. Fairs or circuses at which broadsides or sheet music are offered for sale have served as agents for diffusion in recent times, and so have itinerant vendors and entertainers of all kinds. *Young Charlotte* was probably given its impetus by its author as he journeyed from Vermont to Ohio and thence to Illinois, on his way westward, singing and selling his song as he went. Songs learned at school or in childhood stay in the memory with especial tenacity. Some of the texts of *Jesse James* were said by their singers to have been learned by them as school children, while others said that they had learned the song from farm-hands. Country newspapers have preserved many well-cherished pieces later pasted into scrap books which have been handed down. And, though rarely, song-lovers still copy favorite texts into scrapbooks, as in Elizabethan days. Wandering concert troups, Chautauqua singers, and minor singers of all types, stage stars especially, are great agents in popularization. The once popular negro minstrels helped to universalize many songs, like *Old Black Joe* and *My Old Kentucky Home,* and real negro singers like the Jubilee Singers and the Hampton Institute Singers have kept alive many songs. Those familiar stage and parlor songs of the 1890's, *After the Ball* and *Two Little Girls in Blue,* the first of which was popularized all over the country by May Irwin and other singers, in Hoyt's farce, *A Trip to China Town,*[19] are still vigorous on Western ranches and in villages here and there, though they have long been dead in the circles and places where they emerged. *Shortened Bread,* which still has

[19] See C. K. Harris, *How to Write a Popular Lyric,* 1906.

wide currency in folk-song, among both whites and negroes, was one of Blind Boone's songs. *Johnny Sands* belongs to the first half of the nineteenth century. It achieved enormous vogue by forming part of the repertory of the Hutchinson family, the Continental vocalists, and other singing troupes. It was printed in 1847. A striking melody, or a striking text or story, usually a personal story, given some strong impetus in diffusion, will linger in the folk-memory for decades, when not the faintest consciousness of its provenance remains. As with importations from the Old World, so with indigenous folk-songs, a piece telling a sensational story, or turning on some comic situation, or built about some striking refrain, outlasts songs of other types.

III — THE SOUTHWESTERN COWBOY SONGS AND THE
ENGLISH AND SCOTTISH BALLADS

That a body of folk-song exists in America which supports the theory of " communal " origin for the English and Scottish popular ballads is an idea which has made considerable headway since it was advanced not many years ago. Several writers have found analogy between the conditions attending the growth of cowboy songs in isolated communities in the Southwest, and the conditions under which arose the English and Scottish popular ballads. Said Mr. John A. Lomax, in a paper given by him when retiring president of the American Folk-Lore Society, at its annual meeting, " There has sprung up in America a considerable body of folk-song called by courtesy 'ballads,' which in their authorship, in the social conditions under which they were produced, in the spirit which gives them life, resemble the genuine ballads sung by our English and Scottish ancestors long before there was an American people" . . . "*The Ballad of the Boll Weevil* and *The Ballad of the Old Chisholm Trail,* and other songs in my collection similar to these, are absolutely known to have been composed by groups of people whose community life made their thinking similar, and present valuable corroborative evidence of the theory advanced by Professor Gummere and Professor Kittredge concerning the origin of the ballads from which come those now contained in the great Child collection." [20]

This view was first put forward by Mr. Lomax, who is the chief collector of Southwestern folk-song, in the introduction of his *Cowboy Songs*.[21] He notes when speaking of western communities, how " illiterate people and people cut off from newspapers and books, isolated and lonely — thrown back on primal resources for entertainment and for the expression of emotion — utter themselves through somewhat the same character of songs as did their forefathers of perhaps a thousand years ago." Professor Barrett Wendell [22] suggested that it is possible to trace in this group of American ballads " the precise manner in which songs and cycles of songs — obviously analogous to those surviving from older and antique times — have come into being. The facts which are still available concerning the ballads of our own Southwest are such as should go far to prove or to disprove many of the theories advanced concerning the laws of literature as evinced in

---

[20] Published in the *Journal of American Folk-Lore,* vol. 28, January-March, 1915. For the quoted sentences, see pp. 1 and 16.

[21] New York, 1910. Second edition, 1916.

[22] *Cowboy Songs.* Introduction.

the ballads of the Old World." Ex-President Roosevelt affirmed in a personal letter to Mr. Lomax [23] that " there is something very curious in the reproduction here on this new continent of essentially the conditions of ballad-growth which obtained in mediæval England."

The parallel felt by these writers is worked out with more specific detail and greater definiteness by Professor W. W. Lawrence, in a passage prefixed to a discussion of the ballads of Robin Hood : —[24]

These men living together on the solitary ranches of Texas, Arizona, or New Mexico, have been accustomed to entertain each other after the day's work is done by singing songs, some of which have been familiar to them from boyhood, others of which they have actually composed themselves. . . . These cow-boy ballads are not the expression of individuals but of the whole company which listens to them, and they are, in a very real sense, the work of other men than the author. . . . The author counts for nothing, it will be observed; his name is generally not remembered, and what he invents is as characteristic of his comrades as of himself. . . . Here we have literature which is a perfect index of the social ideals of the body of men among whom it is composed, literature which makes no pretense to literary form or to the disclosure of the emotions of any one man as distinguished from his fellows. There are few communities of the present day which are as closely united in common aims and sympathies as these bands of Western cowboys, hence there are few opportunities for the production of verse which is as truly the expression of universal emotion as are these songs.

Such Western ranches reproduce almost perfectly the conditions under which the English and Scottish ballads were composed.

[23] *Ibid.* Prefixed letter, dated from Cheyenne, 1910. See also Professor Charles S. Baldwin, *English Mediæval Literature* (1914) p. 19.

[24] *Medieval Story.* New York, 1911.

It is obvious from these passages that their writers find a real parallel between the conditions leading to the the growth in our own time, in certain homogenous communities of the Southwest, of fugitive folk-pieces like those gathered by Mr. Lomax, and the conditions responsible for the rise in the Middle Ages of the traditional ballads of England and Scotland. It is the belief that certain types of American folk-song support the theory of " communal" composition of " genuine" English and Scottish ballads, as expounded in many places by Professor Gummere and Professor Kittredge, a belief upheld by their Harvard disciples, Mr. Lomax, Professor Walter Morgan Hart,[25] Professor W. W. Lawrence, and by others. That ignorant and uneducated people may fairly be said to have composed, or had a part in composing, some of the cowboy, lumberman, and negro songs, is held to be evidence that ignorant and unlearned peasants or villagers composed, or had a part in composing, the English and Scottish popular ballads, or at least that they established the type.

A good case can be made out, from examining such material as Mr. Lomax has cited or published, to exactly the contrary effect — namely that the American pieces which he finds to be communally composed, or at least to have emerged from the ignorant and unlettered in isolated regions, afford ample testimony, in structure, technique, style, and quality, that the English and Scottish popular ballads could *not* have been so composed, nor their

[25] *Ballad and Epic* (1907), *Harvard Studies and Notes in Philology and Literature,* vol. IV. See also *Publications of the Modern Language Association of America,* vol. 21 (1906), and *English Popular Ballads,* 1916.

type so established. Here, in summary, are the leading reasons for this affirmation: —

First. The greater part of Mr. Lomax's material in his *Cowboy Songs* did not originate among the cowboys but migrated among them, brought from different parts of the United States, or from the Old World. Especially, the better pieces among them are those most certainly not indigenous to the Southwest.

Second. The pieces which may fairly be said to be of spontaneous cowboy improvisation are not and never will become real ballads, lyric-epics, or stories in verse. They are easily the weakest and most structureless pieces in the collection. They have won and will win no diffusion; and many are probably already dead. Certainly they stand no such chance of survival as do certain pieces, not of communal origin, which have drifted to the Southwest from elsewhere, commended themselves to the folk-consciousness of that region, and retained vitality there as in other parts of the country.

Third. Even the pieces which may be called genuine cowboy pieces are no doubt largely adaptations, echoes of some familiar model, or built on and containing reminiscences of well-known texts or airs. For the most part they may be termed " creations " in a qualified sense only.

Fourth. In general, real communalistic or people's poetry, composed in the collaborating manner sketched out by Professor Gummere and Professor Kittredge,[26] is too crude, too structureless, too unoriginal, too lacking in

---

[26] By Professor Kittredge in Introduction to *English and Scottish Popular Ballads*, pp. xxiv–xxvii. 1904. By Professor Gummere in many books and articles.

coherence and in striking or memorable qualities, to have much chance at survival.   If a piece is to win wide currency, to become fixed in the folk-memory, or get beyond the locality which produced it, it must have strong impetus behind it.   This may come through its peculiar timeliness, or through its preoccupation with a notable personality.   It may come as a result of tunefulness, a memorable story, or striking style, or, again, through some especially potent method of diffusion.[27]   But the impetus must be present if the piece is to get itself remembered, and to make its way over the country as a whole. Most of these qualities are what the well-attested communal improvisations, or creations, those upon which we can place the finger, always lack.   They have little chance at securing the momentum necessary to " float " them, as compared with the songs of the old-time itinerant negro-minstrels,— for example, " Old Dan " Emmett's, Buckley's, the Ethiopian Serenaders', the Fisk Jubilee Singers',[28]— or even as compared with such popular par-

[27] The Ulster ballad, *Willie Reilly*, which has gained considerable diffusion in this country, owed its wide currency to the circumstance that it was adopted as a party song.   For the mode of diffusion of various other pieces, see p. 213.

[28] Some idea of their vogue may be had from Brander Matthews's article, " The Rise and Fall of Negro Minstrelsy," *Scribner's Magazine*, June, 1915.

Some of the popular old-time minstrel songs have been ritualized into, or utilized as game-songs, or " play-party " songs, as the now widely diffused *Old Dan Tucker*, by Daniel Emmett, or *Angelina Baker*, by S. C. Foster, or many others.   See Mrs. L. D. Ames, " The Missouri Play-Party," Goldy M. Hamilton, " The Play-Party in Northeast Missouri," and E. F. Piper, " Some Play-Party Games of the Middle West," printed respectively in *The Journal of American Folk-Lore*, vols. XXIV, XXVII, and XXVIII.   Some of the English and Scottish ballads sung in America have been similarly ritualized.

lor airs as *Juanita, Lorena,* or to songs borne onward by
some notable contemporary event, as was *A Hot Time* by
the Cuban War, or *Tipperary* by the European War.
Suppose that a piece communally improvised did win
stability once in a while, the instance would be a rare case
as over against the folk-songs in established currency
which did not so originate. But who (and Mr. Lomax
has not) has certainly, not conjecturally, pointed out for
America a *good* ballad, *i. e.,* verse-story, which did orig-
inate communally and has also obtained widespread dif-
fusion?

Fifth. A hypothesis is surely questionable which sets
up as standard-giving for the form, type, and genuineness
of the mass of folk-pieces, and as accounting for their
quality and diffusion, a mode of origin responsible, not
for folk-song in general, but at most for a few highly ex-
ceptional instances.

It is time to examine a few well-attested communal
pieces and to note what they are like. A certain percent-
age of the songs in the collection of Mr. Lomax are per-
haps genuine cowboy pieces approached from almost any
point of view. Those which are most typical are related
very closely to the life of the communities which origin-
ated and preserved them. Some of these, the editor tells
us, the singers themselves composed. There are songs
dealing with the life of the ranch, of the trail, songs
of stampedes, of the barroom; but chiefly they deal
with cattle and the cowboys who have them in charge.
There are a few passing references to their "bosses";
but songs which pertain to these, or to the ranch owners,
songs of the lives of their employers or their families, do

not appear.   A few preserve the style of the ultra-senti-
mental or " flowery " period of American verse,[29] with
doubtfully Westernized settings, a few are ascribed to per-
sonal authors,[30] and some are plainly built on or out of
well-known songs.   Of what may be termed the real cow-
boy pieces the following verses, cited as representative by
Professor Lawrence also, will give a good idea: —

I'm a rowdy cowboy just off the stormy plains,
My trade is girting saddles and pulling bridle reins,
Oh, I can tip the lasso, it is with graceful ease;
I rope a streak of lightning, and ride it where I please.
My bosses they all like me, they say I am hard to beat;
I give them the bold stand off, you bet I have got the cheek.
I always work for wages, my pay I get in gold;
I am bound to follow the longhorn steer until I am too old.
>   Ci yi yip yip yip pe ya.

Or —

Come all you jolly cowboys that follow the bronco steer,
I'll sing to you a verse or two your spirits for to cheer;
It's all about a trip, a trip that I did undergo
On that crooked trail to Holbrook, in Arizona oh.

Or —

>   Bill driv the stage from Independence
>   Up to the Smokey Hill;
>   And everybody knowed him thar
>   As Independence Bill.—
>   Thar warn't no feller on the route
>   That driv with half the skill.

The song specificially cited by Mr. Lomax, in his article,[31]

---

[29] *By Markentura's Flowery Marge*, p. 224; or the story of
Amanda and Young Albon, p. 271.

[30] *Night-Herding Song*, p. 324; or *The Metis Song of the Buffalo
Hunters*, p. 72.

[31] *Journal of American Folk-Lore*, XXVIII, cvii, p. 16.

as certainly of communal composition is *The Old Chisholm Trail,* a text of which is printed in his *Cowboy Songs.*[32] Here are its final stanzas:

"I went to the wagon to get my roll,
To come back to Texas, dad-burn my soul.

"I went to the boss to draw my roll,
He had it figgered out I was nine dollars in the hole.

"I'll sell my outfit just as soon as I can,
I won't punch cattle for no damned man.

"Goin' back to town to draw my money,
Goin' back home to see my honey.

"With my knees in the saddle and my seat in the sky,
I'll quit punching cows in the sweet by and by."

The rest of the piece is of the same pattern, or at least is no better. Few would dispute its cowboy composition.[33] Probably it too follows some model; but it is

[32] It should somewhere be said of *Cowboy Songs* that it was obviously put together rather with an eye to the picturesque and effective than with an eye to affording material for the solution of problems in literary history. Mr. Lomax points this out when he terms it "frankly popular." He seems to have drawn on sources of all kinds for his materials.

[33] Usually local individual claims to the authorship of popular pieces of much diffusion should be accepted with especial caution. Those having practical experience in the collection of folk-songs need not be reminded that many pieces are claimed as of individual composition, in outlying regions, which had no such origin — unless for certain added personal tags, insertions, manipulations, or localizings. Mistaken affirmations of authorship are very common. For example, *Starving to Death on a Government Claim,* which has, and has had, considerable currency in the central west, was volunteered, as of his own recent composition, to a collector by a Dakota lad of

plainly enough the work of some one uneducated and untrained. It is crude, without structure or clearly told story, is flat and vulgar in language, and is without striking or memorable quality. It has not a single mark of the "good," or "genuine" ballads of the Child collection, supposed to have won their type, their peculiar quality and worth, from the very humbleness of their composers.[34] *The Old Chisholm Trail* is not and never will be anything like a Child ballad, or like any other memorable ballad. It is just about what we should expect from cowboy improvisation. Yet it is a piece definitely pointed out as furnishing "corroborative evidence."

The songs in Mr. Lomax's collection which do have memorable quality and have shown vitality, which afford the truer analogy for the Old World pieces, are of the type of *Young Charlotte, The Dying Cowboy, The Lone Prairie, The Little Old Sod Shanty,* and for these such composition cannot be claimed.[35]

Our Western cowboys are at least as intelligent and as

fifteen; and his authorship was accepted by his community. Yet all he had contributed was the localizing of a few names. *Breaking in a Tenderfoot*, reported to the present writer as of local composition near Cheyenne, proved to be a rather weak variant of the well-known *The Horse Wrangler*, too weak and garbled to have been by any chance the original text. A teacher once gave the present writer the familiar counting-out formula, "Wire, briar, limberlock, Three geese in a flock," etc. (really an importation from the Old World), as certainly of her own creation in childhood; — this in the sincere belief that it had so originated.

[34] It is well to remember that not all humble composers are by any means either so unskilled or so wholly uneducated that expressions like "artistry" or "conscious authorship" are out of the question when their creations are considered. Burns himself was a ploughboy, the son of a peasant farmer.

[35] For their origin, see pp. 207–209.

generally gifted as the mediæval peasant throngs who are supposed to have created the Old World ballads, and they make a more homogeneous community. When we note what they can do and are asked to believe what the mediæval peasants did — for the older the Child ballads the better the quality — we meet insurmountable difficulties. The evidence offered for the supposed communal origin of the Child ballads is not "corroborative" but the contrary. We know definitely what is the best that the cowboys can do; but when we compare their products with the Child ballads there is almost unbelievable discrepancy.

One other piece has been definitely stated by Mr. Lomax to be certainly of communal origin, the negro song *The Boll Weevil.* It originated in the last fifteen years, he says, and was composed by plantation negroes. He quotes but one verse of it.

> "If anybody axes you who writ this song
> Tell 'em it was a dark-skinned nigger
> Wid a pair of blue-duckins on
> A-lookin fur a home,
> Jes a-lookin fur a home."

Apparently the *Ballet of the Boll Weevil* is a loose-structured, shifting, drifting sort of piece, having like *The Old Chisholm Trail,* nothing in common with "good" ballads, and not likely to have. It is very much what we should expect of a song which emerged from unlettered negroes. And one would like to inquire whether it still lives, flourishes, and shows promise of improvement,[36] or whether it is already dead?

[36] What songs will persist among the negroes? After hearing the Tuskegee or the Hampton Institute singers, one feels that *My Old Kentucky Home, The Swanee River, Old Black Joe,* and some of the

Once more, the very pieces pointed out as giving corroborative evidence are among the weakest in Mr. Lomax's collection. Always those upon which we can place the finger as pieces in the composition of which the folk had part are those relatively weak and flat, giving no promise of a future. The communal pieces generally have no definite narrative element, and they have neither the structure nor the poetic quality of the lyric-epics that constitute the Child collection. If a piece which is of folk-composition may occasionally show this poetic power it is because it adapts or follows closely some good model. But in such case it could hardly be said to be wholly a folk-creation, or to owe its good qualities precisely to the "folk" share in its creation. Once more, too, why should we suppose that human ability has so fallen since the middle ages that untaught throngs could then outdo the best produced by similar throngs upon which we can place the finger nowadays? If we keep our eyes on the evidence, the Child pieces are by far too good to have had

comic songs of the older minstrelsy will have a far better chance at lingering among them than will the inconsequent creations emerging from the "communal improvisation" of the negroes themselves.

It is of interest to find among the songs and fragments of songs collected from the country whites and negroes of the South (see "Songs and Rhymes from the South," by E. C. Perrow, *The Journal of American Folk-Lore*, April–June, 1915), fragments or stray stanzas to be found in, and probably "floated" by, G. W. Dixon's *Zip Coon* (viii, 69), joined with a verse of T. Rice's old minstrel song *Clare de Kitchen*, Stephen C. Foster's *Camptown Races*, or *Gwine to Run All Night* (vi, 16), *De Boatman's Dance* (vii, 26) sung by the Ethiopian Serenaders, and the former minstrel favorites *Lucy Neal* (viii, 62) and *Lucy Long* (viii, 70). The one-time popular song *I'll Not Marry at All* is represented in many stanzas, and there are bits of other popular songs, of Mother Goose rhymes, and of glee club and college songs.

their origin in any way parallel to that which produced *The Old Chisholm Trail* and *The Boll Weevil.*

Before leaving the matter of corroborative evidence, it may be well to bring up more support for the statement that the bulk of Mr. Lomax's pieces are not of cowboy composition but immigrated among the cowboys. *Young Charlotte, The Dying Cowboy, The Lone Prairie, The Little Old Sod Shanty, The Rattlesnake,* are not of cowboy composition but are immigrants. *Bonnie Black Bess* tells of the deeds of Dick Turpin, the highwayman, and is an Old World piece; and so are *Fair Fannie More, Rosin the Bow, The Wars of Germanie,* and *Love in Disguise. The Old Man Under the Hill* is a variant of a Child ballad.[37] *Jack Donahoo* tells of an Australian highwayman and is obviously imported. *A Rambling Cowboy* and *Lackey Bill* seem to be the same piece, and to be identical with E. C. Perrow's *When I Became a Rover,* also of Old World importation.[38] As for *The Railroad Corral,* which might seem so certainly a cowboy song, except that it is so well done, Mr. J. M. Hanson, writing from Yankton, South Dakota, to the *Literary Digest,* April 25, 1914, says that it was written by him to the tune of Scott's *Bonny Dundee,* was originally published in *Frank Leslie's Magazine,* and may be found in republished form in his *Frontier Ballads.* Mr. Hanson was somewhat surprised to find his poem counting as " folk-song." Another piece well executed for folk-song and dealing apparently with genuine cowboy material is *The Ride of Billy Venero.* But this, with a few localizings and adaptations, is unmis-

---

[37] No. 278.

[38] " Songs and Rhymes from the South," *The Journal of American Folk-Lore,* April–June, 1915, p. 161.

takably *The Ride of Paul Venarez* by Eben E. Rexford. Mr. Rexford also might well have felt surprise that his spirited narrative should count as anonymous folk-song. *The Ride of Paul Venarez* had wide currency, after its original publication in *The Youth's Companion,* and was long a favorite with reciters. Another striking piece is *Freighting from Wilcox to Glebe,* having the burden " And it's home dearest, home, and it's home you ought to be," of W. E. Henley's *Falmouth is a Fine Town* (*Poems,* 1886), which in turn derived its refrain from a song by Allan Cunningham. *Whoopee-Ti-Yi-Yo, Git Along Little Dogies* owes its melody and the opening lines to *The Cowboy's Lament* of some pages earlier, which, as Mr. Phillips Barry has pointed out, is an Old World song adapted to plainsmen's conditions. *Buena Vista Battlefield* was a favorite parlor song, and is not of cowboy composition. *The Boston Burglar, Macaffie's Confession, Betsy from Pike, Jesse James, The Days of Forty-Nine,* and many other of the most interesting and widely current or memorable pieces, cannot be claimed as indigenous to the Southwest (nor is this claim made for them); nor is there any real proof that any one of them is of communal composition. Many are not ready to concede such origin for them. The influence of Irish " Come all ye's " and of death-bed confession pieces is strong on pretty much the whole of Mr. Lomax's collection; and there are abundant reminiscences of well-known pieces, as *We'll Go no More A-Ranging* (compare Byron's *We'll Go no More A-Roaming,"* itself a reminiscence), or *The Last Longhorn,* reminiscent of *Bingen on the Rhine.*[39]

[39] Adaptation of something familiar is the first instinct in popular improvisation. Two recent examples from Nebraska may be

Among the pieces cited by Mr. Lomax in his address before the Folk-Lore Society is *Unreconstructed* (included in *Cowboy Songs* under the title *I'm a Good Old Rebel*), which he cites as a " rebel war song," with the suggestion cited. Well-known among the homesteaders of the Sandhill region is *The Kinkaider's Song*, which tells of their life, and celebrates Congressman Moses P. Kinkaid, the author of the homestead law. The piece is built on and sung to the tune of *My Maryland*. For a second example, let an Omaha paper of July 7, 1915, be quoted:

" Joe Stecher, like the heroes of old, is now depicted in ballad. True, it is ragtime, and parody, at that, but ballad nevertheless it is. Here's one they're singing around cafés, using the music of *I Didn't Raise My Boy to Be a Soldier*:

> Ten thousand fans out to Rourke Park went;
> They will never go there again.
> Ten thousand mat bugs' hearts are aching
> From the sight of Cutler's gizzard breaking.

> They all saw Joe Stecher,
> They all dough had bet.
> So through their sobs
> We heard them cry:

> They didn't raise Kid Cutler to be a wrestler:
> They brought him up to be a real guy's toy.
> Who dares to place a foot on the mattress
> And spill our darling Joe-y?

> Let would-be wrestlers arbitrate their troubles.
> It's time to can that tiresome Bull.
> There'd be no punk bouts today, now that the bunch can see
> That they can't produce a guy to throw our Steche-r-r-r-rr.

There is also a song to the tune of *Ballin' the Jack*, and another to *Wrap Me in a Bundle*."

The Kinkaider's Song and *Joe Stecher* afford quite typical examples of songs which are, more or less, of folk-composition. The former is the more creditable, and was made by some one of better education, while the Joe Stecher pieces are of the same general character and quality as *The Old Chisholm Trail* and *The Boll Weevil*.

that the rebel songs were perhaps superior to those of the same class which were of Yankee origin. But this " rebel war song," or " cowboy song," is one of the best poems of Innes Randolph (1837–1887) who was for a time connected with the *Baltimore American*. Mr. Randolph wrote the song to satirize the attitude of some of his elders. A text of his poem, from which Mr. Lomax's folk-piece has lost but a few lines, is accessible in *The Humbler Poets*.[40] A volume of Mr. Randolph's verse was published after his death, edited by his son Harold Randolph.

Another piece cited which is of high quality is *Silver Jack;* and it tells a complete story dramatically; but *Silver Jack*[41] sounds, as Mr. Lomax points out, suspiciously like newspaper verse. It is not the work of one crude and uneducated but of an author trained and skilful. Similarly with a second piece, which is of better quality; it shows skilful use of dialect spelling and relative sophistication.

But is it likely that any of these pieces will live, or win foothold in other regions?

[40] A collection of newspaper and periodical verse, 1886–1910, edited by Wallace and Frances Rice. Chicago, 1911. See p. 322.

[41] A newspaper clipping of this piece, having as title *Jack the Evangelist*, is pasted in a scrap-book of newspaper verse made between 1885 and 1900 by N. K. Griggs of Lincoln. Mr. Griggs was the author of *Lyrics of the Lariat*, *Hell's Canyon*, and later unpublished verse, and it is possible that he composed *Silver Jack*. His wife and his daughter, Mrs. H. B. Alexander, recall his frequent recitation of it, but hesitate to pronounce it his, since the newspaper verses in the scrap-book are unsigned. *Silver Jack* has been found in Iowa, according to E. F. Piper of Iowa City, as well as in Michigan and Texas. He says that he has heard it attributed to the late John Percival Jones, United States Senator from Nevada. To Professor Piper is owed the identification of *The Ride of Billy Venero* with Eben E. Rexford's poem.

"I've been in rich men's houses and I've been in jail,
But when it's time for leavin' I jes hits the trail;
I'm a human bird of passage and the song I trill
Is ' Once you get the habit why you can't keep still.' "

That is verse of the school of the newspaper or dialect poet, not of the composition of the unlettered.

That a song is current in a certain community, or liked by a certain class, is not testimony that it originated among those who sing it, but pretty nearly the contrary.[42] It may have found its way among them in some such manner as *The Railroad Corral* and *The Little Old Sod Shanty* found their way among the cowboys; or as *Casey Jones* and *Life's Railway to Heaven* have been adopted by railway people.

To reiterate, in the body of Western American folk-song, the pieces of proved vitality, most compact in structure and affording the truest analogy to the Child ballads, are not those which are the work of uneducated people of the Middle West or the South, in spontaneous collaboration. The few rough improvisations which we can identify as emerging from the folk themselves,— which we

[42] The songs of a new community usually enter by way of immigration. See, as a random example, *Jamaican Song and Story*, collected and edited by Walter Jekyl. Appendices, *Traces of African Melody in Jamaica*, C. S. Myers, *English Airs and Motifs in Jamaica*, Lucy E. Broadwood, London, 1907. The testimony of Mr. Myers (p. 284) is that: "The majority of Jamaican songs are of European origin. The negroes have learned them from hearing sailor's chanties, or they have adapted hymn tunes." And Miss Broadwood (p. 285) writes to the same effect. "By far the greater part of the Jamaican tunes and song-words seem to be reminiscences or imitations of European sailor's chanties of the modern class; or of trivial British nursery jingles, adopted as all such jingles become adopted."

actually know to be the work of unlettered individuals or throngs, — are those farthest from the Child ballads in their general characteristics. The pieces cited specifically as " corroborative " are inferior, will soon be extinct, and offer no dependable evidence.

IV — BALLAD MAKING AS A " CLOSED ACCOUNT "

A final affirmation to be examined is that there " will be no more ballads," that " ballad-making is a closed account." The following, added to an interesting and well-written discussion of the mediæval ballads, is a typical statement. " True ballads lasted long after the middle ages, but mainly by repetition or modification of those already made. With every century the chances for a new ballad were fewer, until now the ballad has long been extinct as a form of composition. There will be no more ballads; for the conditions under which they are produced are long passed." [43] " Conditions favorable to the making of such pieces," said Professor Gummere, " ceased to be general after the fifteenth century." The same scholar remarked in many places that " Ballads can not be made now, at least among civilized races,"

[43] C. S. Baldwin, *English Mediaeval Literature* (1914), p. 243. And so Professor Kittredge in his introduction to the Cambridge *English and Scottish Popular Ballads* (1904): " Ballad-making, so far as English-speaking nations are concerned, is a lost art; and the same may be said of ballad-singing." In 1915 he wrote (C. Alphonso Smith, " Ballads Surviving in the United States," *The Musical Quarterly*, January, 1916) that if he were again summing up the facts he would modify his statement that ballad-singing is a lost art, either in Great Britain or in the United States, evidence for its survival having come in in the last decade; but the statement that ballad-making is a lost art he did not modify.

that " under modern conditions, ballad-making is a closed account." [44] Statements to the same effect by many others might be cited.

Unless *style* determines what are genuinely ballads and what are not, the making of ballads, *i. e.,* short verse-narratives of singable form, is not a closed account; and there is no reason why it ever should be such. Nor is the making of " popular " or " folk " ballads extinct, meaning by this short lyric tales apparently authorless, preserved among the people, and having an existence which has become purely oral and traditional. The mode in ballad-making has changed and will change. There will be no more Child ballads, for they preserve a style established in bygone centuries. But styles change in folk poetry as they do in book poetry. There is a " history of taste " for folk poetry just as for book poetry. There are as great differences between the folk poetry of the sixteenth and the twentieth centuries as between the book poetry of the sixteenth and the twentieth centuries. Folk poetry is not a fixed thing to rise and die but a shifting thing. The test of what may be termed folk-songs or folk ballads should not be the retention of a mediæval style, and certainly it should not be some hypothetical communal-mystic manner of origin. They are folk-songs if the people have remembered them and sung them, if they have an existence apart from written sources, and if they have been given oral preservation through a fair period of years. As pointed out earlier, in treating balladry in America, attempts at differentiating traditional song into " popular

[44] *The Cambridge History of English Literature,* vol. II, xvii, p. 448; *Old English Popular Ballads,* p. xxvii; *The Popular Ballad,* pp. 16, 337, etc.

songs," or songs made for the people, and " folk-songs " or songs made by the people, based on some hypothesis of distinctive origin or distinctive style, are undependable and unwarranted.   Such differentiation is borne out by the study of no body of homogeneous folk-song, whether regional or national.

When we contrast the older and newer in folk song it becomes obvious that the superiority for persistence in the popular mouth belongs with the former; nor is this to be wondered at. The older singer composed for the ear; otherwise his work was vain. The newer writes for the eye, both words and music; instead of professional musicians as agents of diffusion we now have printing. Skill in creating memorable songs is more likely to characterize composition of the first type than of the second. Much in modern song is unsingable and unrememberable; no one can expect it to make a deep impression on the popular mind.   In the fifteenth and sixteenth centuries poets, whatever their class, were likely to be singers too. If we approach popular song from the side of musical history, it is clear enough that contributions to folk-song should be especially rich at a time when the connection between composition and delivery was very close. In the sixteenth century song was as nearly universalized as it is likely to be for a long time to come. Some musical proficiency was demanded of nearly everybody whether belonging to the upper classes or to the lower. The renaissance lyric, words and music, seems to have had its origin in the higher culture of the times but it attained unparalleled   popularity. Acknowledgment that   the period of the English renaissance had the most memorable style in folk-song is not the same thing, however, as acknowledging that only such folk-songs as exhibit this style are "genuine." Conformity to a mediæval style may not logically be insisted upon as a test of what is truly a folk ballad and what is not.

Already there are in America many short narrative pieces current over the country-side, the authorship and the mode of origin of which are lost; and it is these, not the transient improvisations of cowboys or negroes, which form the better analogues for the English and Scottish ballads. From them a selection of texts and variant versions, with notations of parallels and Old World relationships, could be built up that would be of formidable and instructive proportions. Reference is made to pieces like *Jesse James, The Death of Garfield, Texas Rangers, James Bird, Poor Lorella, Young Charlotte, Springfield Mountain, Johnny Sands, Casey Jones,* and other floating stories in verse which were discussed at some length in a preceding section. There will always be, very likely, a body of short narrative poems, their authorship and origin lost, preserved in outlying regions. They will shift in style but they will ever be behind contemporary song modes by a generation or more. The style of present day traditional song over the United States is, on the average, many decades behind that prevailing in contemporary compositions. In eighteenth-century England and Scotland, the discrepancy was naturally much greater. A large body of song in the mediæval style still lingered, alongside pieces on later themes of middle class life, in a later manner, and pieces of contemporary creation. The older style is the more memorable; it was of higher quality and it persisted longer than will its successors. But it should not be a test of the genuineness of a piece as folk-song

that it continues the style of sixteenth or seventeenth cen-
tury popular song — any more than some conjectural
manner of origin should be such a test.

Why, as a general proposition, should something vague
or romantic be so liked, when the origin of folk-poetry is
in question? Is it a heritage from the romanticism of the
period when interest in ballads arose and their origin
was first made the subject of discussion? Here are some
typical sentences from Andrew Lang:

"No one any longer attributes them to this or that author,
to this or that date . . . its birth [the ballad's] from the lips
and heart of the people may contrast with the origin of art
poetry. . . . Ballads sprang from the very heart of the people,
and flit from age to age, from lip to lip of shepherds, peasants,
nurses, of all that continue nearest to the natural state of man.
. . . The whole soul of the peasant class breathes in their bur-
dens, as the great sea resounds in the shells cast up from its
shores. Ballads are a voice from secret places, from silent
places, and old times long dead."

Yet more typical is this from Theodor Storm's *Im-
mensee* (1851), formerly read so often in our schools
that the view it presents was brought before thousands
of student readers each year:

" [These songs] were not made; they grow; they fall out of
the air. They fly over the land like gossamer, hither and thither,
and are sung in a thousand places at once. Our inmost doings
and sufferings we find in these songs; it is as though we had
helped in composing them."

And compare Mr. Lomax's—

" They seem to have sprung up as quietly and mysteriously as
does the grass on the plains."

This is not very solid ground and it is hardly likely that the next generation of scholars and students will linger upon it. Belief in the origin of the mediæval ballads by communal improvisation in the dance, and belief in the extinction, with mediæval conditions, of the ballad as a literary type, seem to the present writer to have emerged from and to belong to a period of criticism which deliberately preferred the vague and the mystical for all problems of literary and linguistic history — mythological explanation of the *Beowulf* story, multi-handed composition of the Homeric poems, mystical theories of the origin of language.   These originate in romance but they readily fade in a literal, anti-romantic period like our own.

To what degree, one is tempted to ask, is the scholarly and critical enthusiasm for ballads of the last hundred years, or more, due to this romantic attitude? But for their fascinating mystery, would the learned world have preoccupied itself, in the same measure, with ballads? Perhaps when the cloud of romanticism overhanging it has vanished utterly, we may again come to look on balladry as did the cultivated world in the days of humanism.

INDEX

237

PRINTED IN THE UNITED STATES OF AMERICA